The Church
and Secular Education

The Church and Secular Education

LEWIS BLISS WHITTEMORE

GREENWOOD PRESS, PUBLISHERS
WESTPORT, CONNECTICUT

Library of Congress Cataloging in Publication Data

Whittemore, Lewis Bliss, Bp.
   The church and secular education.

   Reprint of the ed. published by Seabury Press,
Greenwich, Conn.
   1. Education--United States--1945-   2. Education--
Philosophy. I. Title.
[LB885.W46L48 1978]   377'.1   78-17152
ISBN 0-313-20540-X

Reprinted with the permission of Rev. Andrew F. Wissemann
and Rev. James R. Whittemore

Reprinted in 1978 by Greenwood Press, Inc.
51 Riverside Avenue, Westport, CT. 06880

Printed in the United States of America

10 9 8 7 6 5 4 3 2 1

To my son
James Robinson Whittemore

PREFACE

This book is an attempt to study the effect of the separation of Church and State upon education. It endeavors to show that as a result of this separation there were losses as well as gains which have affected the educational health of this country. The analysis, as will appear, takes a critical turn; but the criticism cuts both ways and has in the background a profound belief both in the Church and in the American public school system.

The field of inquiry is limited, for the most part, to secular and religious education in the first twelve grades. These are the critical years, but for some reason, until recently, less attention has been paid to the problem in this period than in the one succeeding. Yet the solutions found in earlier years will have a marked effect upon the college campus.

Many books and articles have called attention to the faults of our educational system, but not many suggest a possible solution. It has not occurred to the American public that the answer may be found in a new quarter, an answer so obvious that it has been overlooked. The crux of the whole matter lies in the fact that, since the dichotomy in education occurred, it has been taken for granted that the two educational systems have nothing to do with each other, and that any attempt at cooperation paves the way for Constitutional objection.

This book attempts to prove that a new approach to cooperation is possible, an approach which avoids any legal difficulty and, at the same time leads to a higher level of educational accomplishment.

This discussion deals with strategy, not tactics, with long range objectives rather than with immediate difficulties. Many practical questions have not been dealt with here in the belief that if what is proposed is sound, ways and means will be discovered. *Solvitur ambulando.*

I wish to express my thanks to those who have helped me in preparing the manuscript with their suggestions and constant encouragement. I am especially grateful to the Right Reverend Walter H. Gray, Bishop of Connecticut, the Right Reverend James A. Pike, Bishop of California, Dr. Albert C. Jacobs, President of Trinity College, the Reverend Dr. Ed. LaB. Cherbonnier, Head of the Department of Religion, Trinity College.

Lewis Bliss Whittemore

CONTENTS

Preface   vii

CHAPTER 1: *Parallel Lines Do Not Meet*   3

CHAPTER 2: *The Messianic Complex of the Public
            Schools*   16

CHAPTER 3: *Academic Freedom and the Public
            Schools*   30

CHAPTER 4: *An Appraisal of Current Educational
            Philosophy*   42

CHAPTER 5: *Truth Is Personal*   60

CHAPTER 6: *Reclaiming Its Own Curriculum*   74

CHAPTER 7: *Present Imperatives*   90

CHAPTER 8: *Future Objectives*   105

CHAPTER 9: *The Science of Sciences*   118

The Church
and Secular Education

CHAPTER 1

Parallel Lines Do Not Meet

No article in the American creed is more cardinal than that requiring the separation of Church and State with its corollary that there shall be complete religious freedom. This is something new in the history of the world and is one of the great contributions of the American people to civilization. The Christian priest or minister, the Jewish rabbi, and the Buddhist monk are secure in their places of worship and can assemble with their congregations without fear. One can walk down the streets in clerical garb and receive only the friendliest salutations. This doctrine has made us a friendly nation, and religious differences —like differences in personality—have, in a sense, bound us together and made life more interesting.

There are certain areas, however, where the lines of demarcation have not been, and cannot be, sharply defined; and it is here that a difficult balance must be kept. Of these, the most important is in the realm of education. Here, again, we have something new under the sun, for education which used to be the responsibility of the Church has, through the logic of Church-State separa-

3

tion, become dichotomized.[1] Once unified by religious conceptions, it has now been cut in two, leaving the compelling ideas of religion on one side and so-called secular subjects on the other. It is not necessary to review the steps through which this new division of sacred and secular took place; suffice it to say that they were inevitable. However, it was a surgical operation on a living and breathing thing. Education at the time had a heart, a head, nerves, and sinews. The operation was a dangerous one, and the question was really whether the patient would survive. The patient was the nation itself.

This issue of life and death has been in the background from the beginning. In the onrushing life of our country it has been a concealed and latent issue as we have built a vast public school system across the length and breadth of the land. Into these schools we have poured our treasure, and in them we have placed a pathetic confidence. Of late years there have been critical voices but they went unheeded until Sputnik woke us up like an alarm in the night. With characteristic American impetuosity we have now turned on the schools because, for the first time in our history, we are afraid. In all this confusion and tumult we are right about one thing: education is a matter of life and death, and the questions raised concerning it will bear no superficial answer.

This book, therefore, is dedicating itself to the task of

---

[1] For the purposes of this book, the term "Church" applies to the non-Roman communions. The Roman Catholic Church has taken its stand in the matters treated here so that what is said would have no direct bearing on that Church.

exploring what may be the root causes of this national anxiety. It is asking whether or not certain essential values in a sound educational process were not lost when the nation transferred almost the entire burden from one shoulder to the other and, if so, how these values may be recovered.

The Roman Catholic Church has given a very decided answer to this question. So convinced has it been that the very heart and soul of real education is absent under the aegis of the State that it has erected an immense system of private schools of its own. The process is still going on. This Church wants to make sure that the ultimate meanings of life as revealed in the Gospel are integrated with, and serve to unify, all branches of knowledge. It has not as yet produced a modern St. Thomas Aquinas, but it is doing its best to see that for its own people, at least, theology shall still be Queen of the Sciences. Only so, this Church believes, can education produce integrated, wholesome, and powerful personalities. A dichotomy in the educational process induces a cleavage in the soul of man. The Lutherans and other communions are in sympathy with the fundamental position of the Roman Catholics and, on a much smaller scale, have established their own schools.

The non-Roman Church as a whole, however, while recognizing the difficulty, has supported the public schools partly because any other course has seemed impractical and partly because it has believed in the schools as the only way to preserve the democratic attitude. Here, in actual practice, young people of different creeds, social strata, and racial backgrounds can rub elbows. Here is emphasized in fact, as well as in theory, that God has made of one blood all nations of men on the face of the earth. Here is to be found a stand against snobbery in all its various social and ecclesiastical manifestations. So, in supporting the public schools, non-Romanists may claim that they also have powerful religious sanction.

This is not the sum of all the good and positive things that can truly be said about the public school system of the United States. It has had to face enormous problems due to the spectacular growth of the country. Just to give some kind of education to increasing millions has been a herculean task. Education has had to go into mass production both of educated men and women and of teachers. While fault may be found with the product, administrators and teachers have erected the machinery of education over this broad land, and it is of enormous value. Before any word of criticism is levelled against the public school system, recognition should be given to the leaders and the rank and file of teachers who have given and are giving selfless and devoted service. They are doing more thinking about the problems of education than anyone else, as they stand almost aghast before the very magnitude of their task. It should be added that a large proportion of them are earnest Christian people. In finding fault with the system, it should be remembered that no one group can be made a scapegoat. The public schools did not grow overnight, and they are a reflection of the mores of the public at large. We are all in on this.

When all this has been said, we must still recognize

that there are grave problems to be solved. The mere mass of pupils has led to a dilution of standards. "Social promotion" which means, in the last analysis, pushing a child ahead because there is no room behind, allows a student who is unable to do the work to enter college. Besides this drag there is the dead weight of mediocrity which penalizes the superior student and thus creates one of the most pressing and widely recognized problems of education.

If this were all, a tolerable solution might be in sight; but it is not so simple due to competing interests within the nation itself, all of which try to use the schools for their own ends. Labor exerts its influence and so does management, each side of the economic struggle striving to control the curriculum. Every social theory wants to have its dogmas taught in some course or other. The breakdown of the home, particularly in congested areas, makes the powerful social service world eager to have the schools assume the burden properly belonging to the family itself. Seeing the loss of moral fiber in youth, the schools endeavor through classes in ethics to perform a function hitherto the responsibility of the Church and the home. There is a conflict between those who want to see the schools support the *status quo,* and those who want to make the schools agents in social reform. There is the struggle between those who desire to preserve the humanities, and those who feel that science is the thing. Some believe that the emphasis should be on mental discipline and the power to think while others hold that it is more important to teach a vocational skill and to concentrate on social adjustment. Various professional and economic interests have a stake in the vast sums of money poured out by the American people, while politicians swarming around the state departments of public instruction are not unaware of the waters to be drunk from this Mississippi. Textbooks in literature, history, and sociology have to be tailored to the least common denominator in order to meet the objections of various groups. Some classics have been barred, even from school libraries, because sections of the public have not liked them. Only recently the National Association for the Advancement of Colored People has objected to the inclusion of *Tom Sawyer* and *Huckleberry Finn* on the ground that they reflect on the Negro race. All this has hindered academic freedom, except, perhaps, on the college level. It is no wonder that the charge has been made that due to constant tinkering with subject matter, teachers colleges have paid more attention to teaching methods than to the subject matter taught. As has been said, "They teach everything except the one indispensable thing—the love of learning."

But there are still more complications. When education left its ancient home in the Church, it gradually abandoned the Church's metaphysic which had given it meaning, unity, purpose, and direction. The curriculum, before the divorce, had been a simple one by modern standards; but, elementary as it was, it had a soul and it produced great men. As years went on, theorists came to realize that education was falling apart. They were alarmed by the absence of great and compelling conceptions which alone could prevent the fragmentation of the educational process. In short, they realized that the old metaphysic had to be replaced by a new one if disaster were to be avoided.

As one studies modern philosophies of education, he is surprised to find that these men found themselves wrestling with the old problems of theology. Of course, this is not strange after all, for education, say what you will, deals with human beings in life and death. So in their quest for that which would give cohesion and guidance to the whole process, these theorists had to venture to the heart of metaphysical speculation. They had to consider the ultimates: the nature of reality, the nature of man, the permanent and the transitory, the temporal and the (possible) eternal, free will versus determinism, and the final destiny of man and of creation. Some of these men have been humanists with a religious temperament and so have argued for a God and for the existence of values valid for every man. Others, like old Heraclitus, have argued that the essence of life is dynamic change and that, therefore, Truth is spelled with a lower case "t." It is where one finds it and may be outmoded tomorrow; growth and more growth is the answer, the process is the end. Some, therefore, take the authoritarian approach while others, devoted to the doctrine of "presentism" reject the bondage of the absolute. There are endless gradations from one extreme to the other.

While there have been many, and fundamental, disagreements among the secular philosophers about these questions, there has been one area in which they have been as one. Revealed truth, such as the Church claims to hold, is not relevant to the problem. They seek for truth with the aid of human reason. They do not believe that the Truth seeks for them. Man and nature are to be the final measure of all things. The result has been that the Christian theologian and the educational philosopher just do not speak the same language. It is worse than that— the educational philosopher is resentful of anything that savors of an ecclesiastical approach. So far has the child departed from the mother.

Educational philosophers may say with some appearance of truth that the Church is divided about its own metaphysic. This is only partially true. The so-called divisions among the different branches of the Church reside more in the realm of Church government than in the essential verities of the faith. They have to do with secondary matters which are slowly yielding to a vast centripetal tendency in the Church today. The faith stands and, despite heroic efforts, secular philosophers have erected nothing to take its place. There are no controlling conceptions in the educational world today; it is groping in the dark, confused and bewildered. Modern public school education has no soul. It is no wonder that many think that the increasing secularization of American life is, to a certain degree at least, the outcome of the secular spirit of our public school system.

If this is the net result of an educational policy which in its spirit has departed from all theological sanctions, it means that the public school system has gradually allowed itself to become at odds with the deepest spirit of our nation. This cannot be done with impunity, once the issues have been laid bare. It should be remembered that the nation is not the state but is superior to it. Anson Phelps Stokes, in his monumental *Church and State in the United States,* writes as follows:

The difference between the nation and the state should not be forgotten. The nation is the people with their historic backgrounds, ideals and common loyalties considered as a whole; the state is the organization for maintaining order and promoting the common welfare under a duly adopted constitution. In view of some modern tendencies the fact deserves emphasis that although nation and state act and re-act on each other, it is the nation which creates the state and not vice versa. The state should consequently be the servant, the nation the ultimate master. . . . The idea that the state is God or a God cannot be accepted for a moment.[2]

Stokes goes on to say that while the state has to be secular (though this does not mean anti-religious), this nation is a religious nation. As such it expects its public school system to have a religious character and to be nourished by religious ideals. In support of this, Stokes goes on to say:

those who have studied most carefully American education and who realize its secular but not anti-religious character, recognize fully that it grew out of ideas nurtured by the Reformation. It is the child of American Protestantism.

The Commonwealth of Massachusetts was the real birthplace of public school education in this country; and it will be remembered that each little New England town was originally established as a religious republic with the Church in complete control. The elders and deacons of

[2] New York: Harper and Bros., 1950. I, 12, 13. Used by permission.

the churches and the schools were also the selectmen of the town.

This is our heritage as a nation, and as a nation we have the right and duty to inquire into the fundamental philosophy of the public school system. As a nation we have the right to make the public schools give us an account of their ultimate ideals and objectives. We cannot permit them to be at odds with our ultimate faith about the meaning of life.

If asked how this can be done, the answer is that the Church, from a practical point of view, is the nation organized for religious purposes, just as the state is the nation organized for secular purposes. The fact that the Church is on a voluntary basis, like the home, does not alter its fundamental importance and responsibility. It is to the Church, therefore, that the nation must turn if it feels that the public schools have wandered far afield.

The Church, however, has a great deal to answer for. If the public schools have forgotten the Church during the years, it is also true that the Church has forgotten the public schools. With the exception of one large communion, the Church seems to have lost sight of the fact that at one time it was responsible for the whole of education. It has proceeded on its way, occupied with its concerns in a narrower field as if the public schools did not exist. The Church, until recently, has been oblivious to the secular philosophies which were attempting to fill the metaphysical void, and also to the many valuable educational methods evolved in the public schools. It meant nothing that educational psychology was improving teaching methods through a better knowledge of the child. It has seen the community and the state erect teachers colleges, but the Church has not felt that it is just as necessary to have trained teachers of religion as of mathematics. It has seen new schoolhouses erected with every convenience for both teacher and child, but it has never occurred to this ancient institution that even the best trained teachers can do little under the dreadful teaching conditions it has provided. These statements need to be qualified to the extent of saying that in the last twenty-five years there has been a marked awakening and today an improvement can be observed in teacher training, in textbook materials, and in the erection of parish houses with private classrooms. But even now leaders of religious education seem to be unaware that education is a unitary process. They are not concerned with relating what happens to their own children five days in the week with what goes on Sunday mornings. The public school world is to them an unknown world. In other words, religious education, whether poor or good, has proceeded along a line parallel to secular education, and it is the characteristic of parallel lines never to meet. Here and there there has been "cooperation" with the public schools in the matter of released or dismissed time for religious instruction on weekdays, but that does not imply a meeting of minds about common problems. In other words, we are feeling the effects today of that complete mental abdication which the Church made when it surrendered so many years ago all responsibility for so-called secular subjects.

Yet the Church still guards the faith in the living God, that faith which has been the backbone of education for centuries. Therefore it still has the answer to the deepest questions of education. The fact that this answer claims the authority of revelation does not affect its power to fill the enormous vacuum in the educational world. The only question is whether the answer is true, and if so, how the truth can once more make its legitimate claim. At the moment the Church can only speak in halting accents for, just as the lack of theological background has brought confusion to the world of secular education, so its isolation from the academic world has brought the Church intellectual anemia. In other generations the Church was concerned with the total province of the mind. Its leaders in the universities of the Middle Ages were wrestling with intellectual problems and were seeking to relate theology to the whole of knowledge. In early New England the parsons were the educated men and sharpened their intellects in many fields. It never occurred to them that they must confine their teaching to strictly theological subjects; rather they felt that all knowledge was embroidery on the vestments of God. It was all part of a seamless robe. Had the issue been presented to them, we may feel certain that they would not have admitted that mental excursions were in the nature of trespass. As a result, there was a wholeness, an integrity, a robustness about these men because they had not made any mental abdication nor cut the educational robe in two.

No one would argue, of course, that the Church is not free to pursue its studies into any region of knowledge.

The "no trespass" barrier comes from a habit of mind within the Church itself which the separation of Church and State nourished. The issue was not apparent at the time because public education was in its infancy and secularism had not made its claim with so much violence upon the minds of men. The fact remains that, without perhaps realizing what it was doing, the Church abandoned spiritual responsibility for the interpretation of all knowledge when it relinquished its duty of teaching in the classroom. It ceased to exercise its intellectual muscles in the kingdom of God and as a result those muscles atrophied. It confined theology to a narrow band of experience, not allowing it to test its wings in any, but the most limited, flights. The result has been to bring futility into the heart of the Church, comparable to the confusions in the educational world. In our theological schools and in our pulpits we thresh out old straw. Revivals, however impressive, have lost their power. The great and compelling conceptions of the Gospel, which by right should give all knowledge the rich flavor of the Eternal, are wrapped in a napkin. The Church may have turned the world upside down in the early days, but it is certainly not doing so today.

It is evident that the Church must begin to think in much wider terms. Whether it likes it or not, and whether secular educationists like it or not, it is concerned with the whole educational field. The parallel lines must begin to meet. The first step is to emerge from a protected and, therefore, somewhat unreal world and to rub its eyes. Then it must look at what is actually going on.

CHAPTER 2

The Messianic Complex of the Public Schools

For generations the American public has had a blind and uncritical faith in the public schools—a faith that has been, in fact, a sort of religion. Now that the schools are under attack and the mood has changed, people seem to think that reformation can come overnight both in theory and practice. This, of course, is impossible. The schools are big business and have a big-business complex. Like big business everywhere they are well entrenched both philosophically and economically with many special interests involved. Right now the real attitude of the school system is that this tempest will soon blow over.

In the September issue (1957) of *The School Executive* an article appeared entitled "Schenectady Builds a Comprehensive High School." The Council for Basic Education of Washington, D.C., makes the following comments in its October Bulletin (1957):

For years now we have been watching in the slick paper magazines edited for administrative and school boards, the ever increasing lavishness in school construction, but now we have seen the ultimate in magnificence. Here is a school which has a full-sized gym for boys, another for girls, two auxiliary gyms and an intramural gym; an auditorium, band and orchestra rooms, choral room, cafeteria with stage, a retail store and a faculty-student lounge (in our day the faculty and students didn't lounge together). It has shops for the building trades, automobiles, general industry, graphic arts, electricity, wood-working machines and metals; it has rooms marked food, clothing, child development, trade sewing, cosmetology and one marked simply "living" (home and family, no doubt). There are eight business class rooms, six for science, a greenhouse, a ceramics room, two drafting rooms, a guidance room, one room for a nurse and one for a practical nurse. And, believe it or not, all of this has year round air conditioning made necessary, no doubt, by the torrid climate of Schenectady.

In this gigantic service station of a million and a quarter square feet, there are also class rooms for academic subjects, occupying, if we read the plans correctly about 25% of the total space. Those who take the academic program must sweat it out without benefit of air conditioning but each unit of six class rooms has its own double-sized resource room (whatever that may be) and a central courtyard.

The program of this school is based on Ten Imperative Needs of Youth of the National Association of Secondary School Principals which tells us that any discoverable need of young people must be met by the schools.

I quote this because it gives a good example of the school system of this country as big business; it also reveals an attitude. This school is no isolated phenomenon; to a greater or lesser extent it is the kind of school which the state departments of public instruction are undertaking to build in many places. It is the direct result of a theory of education, now dominant in school circles, which minimizes formal instruction in favor of social adjustment. Here we see the school glorifying its own role to the detriment of family, community, and Church.

The philosophy on which this school is built appeals to state departments of Education. Within the last quarter century immense sums of money have poured into the coffers of these departments through the operation of school assistance laws, which were enacted as an attempt to equalize educational opportunity. Every town in the state has to pay a certain assessment into the central treasury to be spent where it is most needed. Money gives power and control, and these the state departments have not been loath to acquire and to use. For the sake of administrative efficiency hundreds, if not thousands, of local schools have been combined into regional schools built more or less along the lines of that in Schenectady. While this consolidation has doubtless been necessary in many cases, in others it has taken schools out of the context and life of their home towns, their sociological value being sacrificed to administrative efficiency. Almost too late, studies are being made of the value of the smaller existing schools which can be organized into cooperative units within a larger system—a program carried out to a certain extent in Rockland County, New York, with marked success.

But many groups have been interested in the way these large appropriations are spent. The builders of busses highly approve of having our young people spend hours on the road each day. Building contractors are satisfied with this way of managing school affairs. It has been a boon to architects. Manufacturers of gadgets of all sorts

have a stake in this approach to education. The attempt
to teach almost every imaginable skill means a lucrative
business for the makers of electrical equipment, heavy
machinery, business machines, kitchen equipment,
beauty parlor rigging, and so on *ad infinitum*. So the
school in Schenectady, and many others like it, represents
big business in alliance with modern educational theory.

In these United States it has been found necessary to
set certain curbs on big business. There are temptations
which go with size and strength, and the temptation of
big business is to seek for monopoly. It has an innate
tendency to reach out and out, to absorb or to crush
smaller enterprises, to expand its horizon to an almost
limitless extent. With Napoleon each victory only opened
up new vistas for conquest, and so big business with each
advance wishes to enlarge its empire still more. However
it may be rationalized, the driving motive is the lust for
power. It took an heroic effort on the part of one man,
Theodore Roosevelt, to start a movement which resulted
in the anti-trust laws, and it is still necessary for the At-
torney General to keep a watchful eye on great concentrations of power.

Obeying this same instinct, the public school hier-
archy as it has grown in influence, has sought to lay hold
on more and more areas of American life. The school
world has developed a messianic complex which con-
ceals from the leaders the fact that they, too, have a lust
for power, even though it may be honeyed over with
pious sentiment. America, as a nation, has the same duty
to curb this overgrown giant as it had to show the trusts

of an earlier day that there were forces in the country which would not brook control of its economic life.

It is doubtless true that the American public itself must share the blame for the grandiose notions of the school world. Our citizens, through the years, have demanded that the schools take over an incredible number of functions, the responsibility for which properly belongs elsewhere. Instead of resisting these mounting pressures, school administrators, in the main, have acquiesced—usually by adding another special course and still another teacher. New courses not only call for new specialists but also for new classrooms, and it has been charged that when educationists give staggering lists of classroom needs, it will be found—if one takes the trouble to investigate, which most people don't—that many if not all of these "desperately needed" rooms are not for teaching basic subjects but for specialties of one sort or another. So the public has offered the messianic crown to the schools, and there has been but little tendency to refuse it. However it came about, this inflated idea of function, this monopolistic tendency, is not only driving the costs of so-called "education" to astronomical heights but is eating into the vitals of true educational procedure.

The public schools should not assume *responsibility* for the moral character of youth. Educators see the need of this sort of thing only too clearly; but the schools are not and cannot be geared to reach the deepest levels of personality which must be touched if moral character is to result. The school cannot possibly make up for the deficiencies of the home during the formative years, nor can it rival the forces of the community, both good and bad, which are such vital factors in personality development. It cannot take the place of the Church. Results have shown that training in good manners, cooperative living, and ethics, even under the best of teachers, do not get to the heart of the matter. Most of our young delinquents are members or graduates of our high schools where they have been exposed to the best that the school has to offer.

Of course, the schools should be on the side of righteousness; what I am saying is that good thinking on the part of educationists and the public would lead to the conclusion that this is a field in which the primary responsibility does not rest with the school system. It should rid itself of this incubus.

The schools cannot be responsible for the family life of America. They can do helpful things for those who want to be helped; they are on the side of good family life; but when it is bad, they cannot reform it. The roots of the trouble go too deep, the forces of environment are too complex, the personality defects too compelling (we are verging on the problem of sin both personal and corporate) for the school with its own peculiar genius and responsibility to handle. The school can neither reform the family life of America nor take its place—this latter the present tendency. Look through the list of courses in a school like the one in Schenectady and you will find that many of them are based on the theory that family life has failed. If this is indeed the case, then we are lost—for this is just not the public school's business. An enormous weight would be lifted from the necks of our educators and a staggering financial burden removed from the American public if the schools would admit that they cannot take the place of father and mother and state flatly that they are not going to try.

If the school cannot reform or replace the home, neither should it feel that it is responsible for reforming the community or the nation. As has been mentioned before (Chapter 1), there is a school of thought among educators which maintains that the schools should take the lead in making over our manners, mores, and politics. Cost what it may in controversy and bitterness, the schools should be in the forefront of the battle. Here is empire building indeed, for these men—perhaps more than any others—have been touched by the messianic delusion. No one denies that the school has the right to inform the public about conditions which interfere with its proper, though limited, function; but this is different from entering the lists where it is totally unfitted to wage combat. Whether the theories of these zealots are conservative or radical, reactionary or communistic, they are calling on the schools to step entirely out of character.

Other empire builders seem to think that the schools should take over the whole field of vocational training. They believe that their job is to provide each student with a skill so that on graduation he may get immediate and lucrative employment. One has only to look at the courses offered in many of our high schools to realize the vastness of this enterprise.

The school men have seemingly strong reasons for such a major operation of the educational army. The first one is that, in spite of the pressure on the colleges, the majority of high school students either quit school at sixteen or thereabouts, or upon graduation. Therefore the theorists say that the course of study for them should not be dominated by a college system into which they will never enter. It seems obvious that the answer is to put the emphasis on getting these young people in line for a good job and to lay less stress on academic subjects. Then it is argued that it does every young person good to learn to do something with his hands as well as with his head. Some manual skill, some ability to deal with physical objects whether they be musical instruments or automobiles, carpentry or drawing, gives a certain assurance and poise in meeting life; it balances the psyche somehow. This is why occupational therapy is so helpful to disturbed patients. Or, again, it is often helpful to have a second string to one's bow, and this secondary skill may save the day when a man loses his primary job as so many did during the great depression.

Still another argument for vocational training is that many of the young people who do not go to college do not like academic subjects anyway. To them high school is simple boredom and for this reason the wise course is to prepare them for a job of some kind even though their academic instruction is decidedly sketchy.

In the background is despair about those American homes in which the atmosphere is decidedly anti-intellectual. There can be no question but what the indifference to mental training on the part of youth stems in great part not from lack of ability but from a parental attitude of indifference and hostility to the things of the mind. These boys and girls live in homes where no books are read, where no interest in the child's program is shown, where no help with the lesson is given, where the teachers are called "eggheads" and where the family ethos is characterized by discord and prejudice. Then there is the attitude of the boy's gang which may have a powerful influence against the school and all that it stands for. In the far background is the fact that we Americans are the most pragmatic people since the Romans; we are for anything which seems calculated to bring obvious and immediate results. It is easy to see how educators can come to feel that by magnifying vocational instruction they are doing the only possible thing in adjusting to the realities of the American scene.

This, I believe, is a fair presentation of the case for teaching in the new jargon of the school world, "the industrial arts." The arguments, in the writer's opinion, are not conclusive. The schools are attempting an impossible task.[1] It has been estimated (I don't know how, but it seems reasonable) that there are 20,000 different kinds of jobs in this country. Even though the present immense expenditure of money and effort were increased manyfold, the schools cannot possibly cover the field. In many cases the school program is not well thought through in reference to actual need. It may prepare electricians in a community where no electricians are needed. In the Wheaton High School, Maryland, a course is offered

[1] See *Schools Without Scholars* by John Keats (Boston: Houghton Mifflin Co.), 1958.

which trains girls how to run a beauty shop. They spend three hours every day on this subject, and at the completion of 1500 hours of work they can take the state examinations for a cosmetology license. The question is whether Wheaton needs 48 hair driers who are graduated each year or whether Maryland, with its many other facilities for this study, can absorb them. It is also a question how many of these girls will want to go into this "profession" anyway; maybe they take the work as a snap course. In any case, this is not *education*. In schools throughout the country boys are taught the printing trade with little regard for the grim realities. The Printers' Union is a strong one, and it limits its membership in order to keep its wages high. As John Keats says,

It is difficult to join a union unless you are related to a printer and in any case printers have set up their safeguards for the quality of their craft. The union requires you to begin a long tough apprenticeship which gives you a thorough training. It also pays you while you learn and has the added advantage of delaying the appearance of journeyman printers on the market.[2]

Again, what the school does is amateurish. It is impossible to duplicate the training that one gets in a factory workshop. For one thing, machinery is so specialized now, even in the same general industry, that it is difficult for the school to duplicate it. If it succeeds, this heavy and expensive apparatus tends to become obsolete almost before it can be installed. Neither the machines nor the work nor the atmosphere of a factory are duplicated. For

[2] *Ibid.*, p. 118. Used by permission.

the most part factories prefer to train their men in their own shops to use their own machines. This is true along other lines. A bank president told me recently that what the girls learned about computing machines in school did them very little good. He much preferred to train them himself on the type of machine used at the bank.

Vocational processes change so rapidly that what is learned in school today may be behind the times tomorrow. Shorthand gives way to steno-typing, to the hush-a-phone or the tape recorder. The old method of card filing is out of date as one must know how to operate indexing machines and how to feed data to mechanical brains. The schools, even with unlimited funds, cannot keep up with this swift process of change. Borderline courses which hover around the edge of vocational training have even less reason for existence. They include dating techniques, proper grooming, cooking, sewing, interior decorating, consumer purchasing, auto driving, how to use the telephone, marital problems, sex education, and even baby-sitting.

All of this is not education, and the responsibility for it rests elsewhere than on the public schools. If the public schools can produce intelligent young men and women who have a sound basic education, they will have made a major contribution to the vocational field. With good material to work with, business can do in a quarter of the time and twice as efficiently what the schools (if they can do it at all) can only accomplish laboriously and at enormous expense. Vacations offer a wonderful chance to get a real job which will train hand as well as head, besides giving contact with reality. Labor unions have their systems of training apprentices. The Army, Navy, and Air Force give on-the-job training in many lines which is really worth something. Here is a resource which the schools do not even consider in mapping out their programs. It is striking how the messianic complex blinds school men to the forces round them in the community, state, and nation which are already doing this kind of work with our young people. There are private schools for interior decoration, for dancing and the ballet. The Little Theatre movement gives young people a chance to act. Private teachers earn their living teaching the violin and the saxophone. There are schools in cosmetology, business practice, and so on without end. These private individuals and schools ask a fee for their instruction which is paid by those who really want their services. Why should this expense be made a charge on the public purse in order that young people may take snap courses instead of learning how to use their minds? The waste of money, motion, and time in this area is staggering; and if the home cannot teach how to dress, how to handle a knife and fork, how to buy a package of cereal at the store, something about sex and married life, we shall just have to lump it and take the consequences. School money should not be spent for this sort of thing because it is none of the school's business.

The Church, as it casts its eye about on the American scene, may begin its gentle criticism with a twofold observation: first, that the great public school bureaucracy should be cured of its megalomania; and second, that the Church should rid itself of its inferiority complex.

Author's Note:

Dr. Conant's *The American High School Today*[3] is a beautiful illustration of the messianic complex in education. At a time when big business is tending to divide into smaller units because of sociological and other factors, Dr. Conant makes an evangelistic plea to reduce the number of high schools in this country from 21,000 to 9,000. Big business has found that by subdividing and placing units in small towns the men can live in more natural surroundings with a home and perhaps a garden. They have normal relations with their neighbors of different sorts in a real community life. They are not likely to be affected by mass hysteria. They are more contented, more interested in the resources of their surroundings, more in touch with nature. Efficiency is not lost because ways have been found to link up the various units. In like manner, high schools can be linked up in a given area to give the utmost efficiency without losing many precious values. Dr. Conant loses sight of many intangibles in his recommendations. In his preoccupation with the idea that formal education in the public schools is the whole of education he gives the impression that no other educational forces exist and that no time need be allowed to the home, church and community. He admits that

[3] James B. Conant. *The American High School Today* (New York: The McGraw-Hill Book Co., 1959).

such huge concentrations may involve an absolute waste of time in bus transportation, possibly up to three hours a day. It all adds up to a complete domination of the pupil's day by the public school. Home, church and community are not directly attacked—they are just calmly eliminated. The incidental fact that bus transportation puts a premium upon the purchase by teenagers of $50 jalopies is not worthy of mention. It is not worthy of notice that the huge high schools which he recommends remove the pupils from vital touch with their own communities and also separate the communities from the schools. Dr. Conant to the contrary, experience has shown that the larger the high school, the less touch the parents have with it. His recommendations, if followed, would mean taking a long step toward the absolute control of education by the state and national government. If this country should ever have a dictator (and it can happen here), he would have, through such consolidation, an ideal instrument for the control of the thought and public opinion of the nation. Dr. Conant's negative feeling toward private schools is an inevitable corollary to his main contention. He would remove freedom of choice from the educational world. Gigantism brooks no rival.

CHAPTER 3

Academic Freedom and the Public Schools

Let us assume, for the purposes of argument, that the public school system has divested itself of its messianic complex; let us assume that the schools have lightened the cargo and have determined to confine themselves to what alone they can do—namely, to give a thorough basic education to the youth of the land—what then?

Some years ago a Mrs. McCollum, an atheist, objected to the fact that in the public schools of Champaign, Illinois, clergymen and religious teachers were allowed to teach religion inside the school building and within school time to those pupils who desired to receive instruction. The case finally went to the Supreme Court which decided in favor of Mrs. McCollum's contention that this was contrary to the constitutional provision bearing on the separation of Church and State. Justice Black voted with the others, but in a subsidiary opinion he gave classic expression to the doubts in his, and many another, mind. The opinion read as follows:

Perhaps subjects like mathematics, physics and chemistry are or can be completely secularized. But it would not seem practical to teach either practice or appreciation of the arts if we are to forbid exposure of youth to religious influences. Music without sacred music, architecture minus the cathedral, painting without the scriptural themes would be eccentric and incomplete even from a secular point of view. Yet the inspirational appeal of religion in these guises is often stronger than in a forthright sermon. Even such a science as biology raises the issue between evolution and creation as an explanation of our presence on this planet. Certainly a course in English literature that omitted the Bible and other powerful uses of our mother tongue for religious ends, would be pretty barren. And I suppose that it is a proper if not an indispensable part of preparation for a worldly life to know the role that religion and religious belief have played in the tragic story of mankind. The fact is that for good or ill nearly everything that gives meaning to life is saturated with religious influences derived from Paganism, Judaism, Christianity both Catholic and Protestant and other faiths accepted by a large part of the world's peoples. One can hardly respect a system of education that would leave the student wholly ignorant of currents of religious thought that move the world society for a part in which he is being prepared.

And how one can teach with satisfaction or even justice to all faiths such subjects as the Reformation, the Inquisition or even the New England effort to found a Church without a Bishop and a State without a King, is more than I know.

This can mean only one thing: that there cannot be academic freedom in the full sense of the word in the public schools of America. Let us attempt to document this by looking at the contents of a typical curriculum in essential education. It will be seen that the amount of freedom varies from course to course, but that in all of them the barriers to a full play of mental activity are present to a greater or less degree.

In mathematics the teacher finds that there are few areas, if any, into which he may not freely venture. He can teach to his heart's content without being on his guard. It is interesting to note, however, that even in mathematics he begins to verge on the ultimate, and we find a mathematician like the late Sir James Jeans suggesting that the universe should be interpreted in terms of mathematics. Here he approaches the metaphysical.

In the sciences dealing with observable and measurable phenomena the teacher also has wide scope, although here too he begins to skirt the boundaries of ultimate meaning. Eddington talks about the possible existence of what he calls "anti-chance," and what is anti-chance but another name for God as Comte du Nouy says? Professor Kreider of Yale used to point out that if it were not for the fact that water expands when it freezes, lakes and rivers would freeze from the bottom up and life such as we know it on this planet would be impossible. The sciences all trail off into the unknown but they can be taught with a good deal of freedom. I cannot see that the teacher of geography would have much trouble; the Miss Doves of the academic world must have a delightful freedom and must teach with abandon. Basic English, written and spoken, can steer clear of ultimates rather easily unless examples of good writing inject them from the sidelines. Youth, we must remember, is not only annoyingly inquisitive but also profoundly theological. However, this subject seems as neutral as any, granting that anything can pop us right into the eternal. The same thing can be said for the teacher of foreign languages.

The need for this is becoming increasingly recognized now that the United States is in more vital contact with so many peoples. The mastery of another language is one of the best means of stimulating mental activity and of introducing one to a very pure joy of the mind. It is truly said that we do not know our own language until we learn another. Words attain a new depth of meaning when we can, as it were, stand off at a distance and look at them. Our own language acquires a new tang and character if we can hear it with the ears of another culture. So, from every angle, let French or German or Spanish or Russian or Chinese be taught early. This last is not so fanciful as it sounds, for a young Chinese friend told me recently that in addition to teaching other courses in a preparatory school in Connecticut, he offers an elective in Mandarin. At the moment he had sixteen boys in the class and they were having the time of their lives actually conversing in Chinese. But I digress. The teacher of languages in a public school can teach with a wonderful freedom.

When we approach other subjects which should be taught in any basic curriculum, we find ourselves in the midst of the difficulties cited by Justice Black. He has already given expression to the impossibility of teaching the fine arts and music without religious reference. In English literature and world history we are in the midst of the tide rip. In this region academic freedom simply does not exist in the public schools of America. The limitations on freedom, therefore, are not confined to the injunction not to teach religion as they come from certain groups who would limit the boundaries of literature or would dilute or misinterpret episodes in history which they believe might reflect on them.

Academic restrictions about subject matter kill the spirit of scholarship as well as put limits to free enquiry. They produce mechanics or technicians in literature and history rather than scholars. Scholarship demands a use and training of the mind which should be one of the great objectives of education. It is about this question of mental training that the Great Dispute is raging today as we have come to the conclusion that our boys and girls are not being taught to think. Scholarship demands an intellectual zeal and if a man must teach "under wraps," he loses the itch for perfection, the incentive toward excellence. What must be the attitude of the teacher who is compelled to perform in a strait jacket? Under such circumstances he must always try to avoid stepping on eggs, he must bypass unpleasant facts, walk safely, hold himself in leash. It would seem that the spirit of independent and free investigation, the impulse to probe deeply into the heart of his favorite subject—in other words, to become a dedicated scholar—would be dampened by the realization that he cannot take his students with him into areas where it really gets exciting to the mind and spirit. There *is* such a thing as the love of learning and a love of the things of the mind, but such raptures do not take place in a controlled and cautious environment. The bald and brutal fact is that the ethos of the public school does not lend itself to the teaching of the great humanities. This lack of academic freedom may be one of the reasons why teachers colleges lay so much stress on method rather than on subject matter— do everything in fact except to inculcate the love of learning. They know only too well that the intellectual life and the power to think are not and cannot be the primary objectives of the schools into which their graduates will go. We may likewise find in this situation the reason why the graduates of liberal arts colleges who wish to make teaching a career, go to private schools or seek for positions on the college level.

With teachers suffering under these handicaps it is not difficult to imagine what the effect is on young people. Intellectually they are being sold down the river. In spite of everything to the contrary, the majority have the power to think and can be aroused by a teacher who is bubbling over with his subject. Then comes the shower of cold water. Let us assume that a good teacher has aroused in his class a real enthusiasm for Shakespeare. For the first time in their young lives there has come a new and enchanting excitement. They have caught a spark of the scholar's zeal; they would like to know about this genius merely for the intellectual satisfaction such mastery would give them. Then they are told that they cannot study the *Merchant of Venice* because of the Jewish problem. Would not this class feel that some outside and alien force had violated its intellectual integrity? Would it not resent the implication that its members cannot be trusted to know the historic fact that this people has been hated here and there throughout the centuries without losing their balance? The reading of this particular play (which incidentally contains one of the most eloquent defenses of the Jew ever written) would serve to start the sluggish machinery of their minds working. But they cannot read this play as a group effort because a timid school board has lowered the boom. The smoking flax is snuffed out; there is no kindling of the fire. Illustrations may be multiplied from many different sources. One superintendent of a public school reported recently that there were thirty different pressure groups in his small town, each one demanding that the curriculum be tailored to meet its demands!

If this deadening process can take place in the teaching of literature, it is still more soul-killing in the teaching of history. School textbooks have been so denatured to please various groups that the life has gone out of them. Such dilution of the real facts about critical historical episodes is an insult to the intelligence of both teacher and pupil. It accounts for the listless atmosphere of many classrooms which might tingle with discussion and mental excitement.

The lack of academic freedom makes it difficult to uncover the deepest meanings and motivations of life. When naturalism seeks to pierce the depths, it leads men farther and farther from the human into an impersonal, drab, and even horrifying wilderness. Science as a method of conquering nature is enthralling; as a tool for exploring meaning, it is beyond its depth. Casserley, in his book *The Christian in Philosophy,* makes the point that the writers of history and literature are more nearly on the right track because they are dealing not with molecules but with man as he is. They are concerned with personalities, with great spirits, with peoples in triumph and disaster, with glorious causes and with forlorn hopes, with heroic devotion and with base treachery. Not in the phenomena of nature, but in the profundities of the soul made in the image of God, do we find the power to catch at the skirts of *That which is*. In this area alone lie the deep inspirations, the flavor of greatness, the intimations of destiny—all of those influences which shape the character and quicken the mind. Here alone are to be found meaning, purpose, direction. Here, if anywhere, one can come upon the Truth that sets men free. Why should we wrap the teachers of such subjects in the grave clothes of academic restrictions? Let them make mistakes, let them arouse controversy, but let them be free. Alas, how vain is such a dream, for the public school world cannot endure teaching like this.[1]

[1] Mr. Robert Lekachman, in "Religion and the Schools" (published by the Fund for the Republic), argues that the doctrine of neutrality in public school teaching is valuable if for no other reason than that the immature child simply picks up the parents half-baked prejudices. The value of neutrality or "openness," he says, is that the schools may counteract parental and local prejudices by teaching that there are two sides to every question and thus help to postpone more mature judgment until a later age.

Apart from the basic theory behind this (that there is no fixed body of truth) one can readily see that the emphasis is on the value of teaching without conviction and thus deprives the teacher of the chance to be and to give himself. One cannot imagine anything more calculated to repress any emergence of intellectual ardor among the students. If the demand today is for education which will make students think, this is certainly not the way to go about it.

The lack of academic freedom, of course, comes to a focus in the relation of the public school to the Judeo-Christian tradition which is the Great Humanity. Here, indeed, we face a difficult problem, for while the division of Church and State as required by our Constitution is a proper one and, in certain ways already described, has brought great benefits, it also confronts education with the enormous difficulty so well described by Justice Black.

To meet this genuine difficulty many are proposing that the schools do not teach religion but *about* religion. It is felt by a good many educators as well as churchmen that there can be in the school system itself a factual or objective presentation of religious matters which will not collide with constitutional provisions and ought not to arouse public opposition. Those who are pressing for this detached presentation of religion claim that without this privilege it is impossible to carry through in many subjects. The center of gravity would still be in literature, history or the like, but the teacher would be free to carry the discussion into religious areas if necessary to explain the subject matter.

In actual practice under present conditions, this impersonal presentation of religious truth offers great difficulties. Even educators who are favorable to the idea are hesitant because they see that from a practical point of view, it would be impossible to secure teachers who are well-trained enough to venture into such regions without disaster. Such teachers, to avoid pitfalls, would have to have the equivalent of a theological school education.

They would have to be thoroughly conversant with the Bible, with Christian history and apologetics. They should know the impact of the Christian faith on philosophy because philosophical questions may arise in any class.

I have heard of one teacher who could do this. In her class at Wellesley College, Professor X taught not only the objective facts about Roman Catholicism, Orthodoxy, Anglicanism, and the various groupings of Protestantism, but she was also successful in imparting the inner spirit. When she was dealing with the Orthodox Church, for instance, it was as though she herself were a member and speaking with all the zeal of a new convert—and so with them all. The class was very successful because each member felt that her faith was given a fair presentation. But where, the educators say, can we get teachers like that? They feel that the system is not capable of producing the teaching power for such a formidable task.

A still further question would arise about the factual presentation of religion even if there were a multitude of teachers like Professor X. I would hazard a guess that a good many students in her classes were eager to know what her own commitment was. Someone has said that the best way to teach philosophy is to be committed to no particular branch of it; the answer to that is that one can teach everything and impart nothing. Pupils in the most brilliantly conducted "objective" class are still searching for a meaning which can be applied to themselves, and so they want to know what the teacher thinks in his heart of hearts. This is the nub of the matter, the milk in the coconut. Did Professor X answer the questions put to her after class? I do not know, but I rather think she did. She had to be *herself*.

Unfortunately, therefore, there are grave, if not insuperable, difficulties in the way of teaching factual religion in the first twelve grades of public school, desirable as such an undertaking might be. In the first place, only a highly trained and specialized teacher can do it well, and such teachers cannot be obtained in sufficient numbers to make any impression. In the second place, these teachers would have to keep their own convictions to themselves or there would be a row. There might be anyway.

So here is the tragedy of it all—academic restrictions in the public schools keep teachers from being fully themselves and yet all great teaching, like all great preaching, demands that the teacher give his very soul along with the course. Only so can there be that impartation of meaning without which factual matter is as dry as the dust of Sahara.

In the report of the Rockefeller Brothers Fund on educational needs which appeared in the *New York Times* on June 23, 1958, one finds the following paragraph:

What most people, young or old want, is not merely security, comfort, or luxury—although they are glad enough to have these. They want meaning in their lives. If their era and their culture and their leaders do not or cannot offer them great meanings, great objectives, great convictions, they will settle for shallow or trivial meanings. People who live aimlessly, who allow the search for meaning to be satisfied by shoddy and meretricious experiences, have simply not been stirred by any alternative meanings, ethical values, ideals of social and civic responsibility, high standards of self-realization.

What then? This was the question at the end of the first paragraph of this chapter. We come back to it and to the doubts expressed by Justice Black. It seems plain that after a lot of excess baggage has been gotten rid of, after the school boards and administrators have raised standards, eliminated social promotion, paid especial attention to the intellectually elite, in other words "got tough," many questions will still remain unanswered. Among them the greatest is "What is the meaning of life?" the public school answer to which we must next consider.

CHAPTER 4

An Appraisal of Current Educational Philosophy

While it is true that no one group in the educational world can be made a scapegoat for present confusions, the fact remains that educational theorists have been men of enormous influence in shaping the form and molding the spirit of education in the United States of America. Some of these men have achieved national fame. All have played a part and in the teachers colleges of our country they have influenced the thinking of the budding instructors of our youth. The purpose of this chapter is to take a closer look at what these leaders have been thinking and teaching, for their ideas have sifted down through the teachers into the classroom and have affected the attitudes of our people.[1]

Most educators, though not all, are agreed that education should be dominated by an over-all purpose which guides and illumines every part of it. As it has been taken for granted that ancient theological ideas should not form the basis of educational objectives, the conception of

[1] See *Modern Philosophies of Education* by J. S. Brubacher (New York: McGraw-Hill Book Co., 1950) for an exhaustive study of this subject.

good citizenship in its various manifestations was seized upon as an alternative. This sounds simple, but in actual practice this approach has been found to bristle with difficulties. Does good citizenship imply the acceptance of the status quo? If not, does it mean that the schools should be instruments of reform? Does good citizenship mean being intelligent about world problems and the role that the United States should play in attempting to solve them? Here, again, there is a difficulty because there is a stronger isolationist sentiment in this country than we realize. It is worthy of note that there has been an effort recently to expunge any reference to the United Nations from the textbooks of this country. The Daughters of the American Revolution have passed a resolution (1958) calling for our withdrawal from the United Nations, stating that the United States should no longer harbor its headquarters on its soil. Within the nation does good citizenship require that one should adhere to the tenets of labor or of management? Of course, the schools can teach the duty of exercising the suffrage and of accepting public office if fitted for the same and duly elected, but good citizenship is not easily defined, and as a conception which will unify the total process of education it has failed.

Recognizing this, educational theorists have been forced into the area of metaphysical speculation, the feeling being that the very nature of things, the cosmic reality so to speak, should be the guide to unifying and controlling ideas. Almost against their will they have been compelled to consider problems which have always been the concern of theology. It is not strange, therefore, that from the very outset of their quest they have found themselves wrestling with questions which have occupied men's minds throughout the centuries. One finds that the major differences between educationists were discussed by the realists and nominalists of the Middle Ages; and while we are likely to think that the arguments of the scholastics were sterile, our opinion changes when we discover that they have a direct bearing on present day theory and practice.[2] The realists believed that, in the ontological sense, there were universals before there were particulars and that the particular is simply the expression of some antecedent and causative universal which gives it character and status. So the general idea of a school preceded the actual construction of a school. The general idea "dog" preceded the creation of any particular dog and gave to the animal his essential "dogness." A universal conception of man antedated (ontologically) the creation of men. Universals of goodness, truth, and beauty brought into being concrete expressions of those qualities. In other words, the realist felt that the universal had objective reality. The nominalists, on the other hand, claimed that all with which we have to do exists only in the particular. They saw that one dog resembled another

---

[2] Philosophical terms change their meaning with the passage of time, and the realist of the Middle Ages was just about the opposite of his modern namesake. In this book we have used the word rather loosely in the medieval sense, as a convenient peg on which to hang a number of philosophic hats. The word "nominalist" is not so much in common use today, but again, it has served as a cover for numerous theories based on naturalism.

and did not object to classification for the sake of mental convenience, but they did object to the conception that there is a univeral dogness. That is an illusion. The thought is abstract, speculative, intangible. Likewise there may be good men, but to think that there is any universal goodness in the structure of the universe which has its expression in good individuals is ridiculous.

This may seem farfetched to the modern mind, but as we go on I think that it will become apparent that the major division among the theorists who set educational policy is along the lines of ancient realism and nominalism. Forced, as I say, to abandon citizenship as an all-embracing ideal, these thinkers have attempted to hit upon the nature of reality—the very essence of things. At this point the question immediately arises as to whether reality is static or dynamic. The educational realists hold that back of changing phenomena there is a changeless reality or universal. In this they have both ancient and modern thinking to brace their argument. Aristotle saw change in plants and animals, but behind the change he postulated a universal and constant cycle which governed change. Einstein postulated an observable universe of unchanging law. So the realists believe that men are the expression of a universal manhood and that man has the capacity to respond to the universal. Up until fifty years ago, the realists held the field.

But the modern realists by no means have the field to themselves today; as a matter of fact they have been steadily losing ground. The nominalists are exceedingly active and very confident. They dismiss the idea of the changeless and universal, as speculative and impossible of proof. The essence of the universe, they say, is change, which we can see on every side with our own eyes. With Darwin they claim that there is no constant cycle which governs change. Species may vanish or be metamorphized into other species. There is not *man,* there are only individual men; and through the process of adaptation and the survival of the fittest, human nature as we know it may be entirely different in the future. There is no universal goodness which brings about goodness in individual men and women. Goodness itself cannot be defined for it varies according to circumstances, and what we call good now may later be called evil. The idea of a universal moral law is nonsense. Morality differs from man to man, tribe to tribe, nation to nation. Truth itself is not universal as it only emerges from time to time as we solve problems. We make truth, and in this emerging world of particulars ungoverned by any universal, the truth of tomorrow may be very different from the truth of today. This is a multiverse, not a universe; it is a churning world of particulars in which anything can happen. So just as the realist approach to education has a certain discipline, so the nominalist approach is flexible.

Many educators, however, despair of basing educational theory and procedures upon ultimate reality which to their mind is beyond human grasp. There seems to be a general agreement that there is an external, objective universe (although some philosophers deny even this), but these men think that the cosmos in itself is essentially unknowable. The only firm basis for educational theory, therefore, must not be the nature of the universe but the nature of man.

Unfortunately, this approach proves to be as precarious as the other. A swarm of questions fly like butterflies out of this Pandora's box. The question immediately arises as to whether human nature is essentially good, or essentially evil, or a mixture of the two. Upon the answer hangs much educational theory. The romantic progressives, following Rousseau, believe that human nature is naturally good and that the instincts are to be trusted. While there is nothing fixed or stable about it, it will respond to reason. Man is just a part of the natural process of birth, growth, decay, and death—like the trees. The idea that he has a soul as a child of God, even though he be fallen from grace, is abhorrent to this school of thought. Man is certainly not conceived as but little lower than the angels; it would be more true to say that he is but little higher than the apes. The ideas of sin, redemption, and such are not scientific; they belong to the mental rubbish of the past and should be thrown into the ash cans of history.

The traditionalist or essentialist approach is from the other end. In distinction to those who try to describe man in terms of nature, the traditionalist describes him in terms of universals which transcend nature. He, therefore, believes in *man*. He may not talk of God, but he does have faith in the compelling power of the unseen which bestows manhood and the power to respond to goodness, truth, and beauty. Deep calls to deep and every man has it in him—call it a soul if you will—which can respond to the changeless and the eternal.

Thus we see that in transferring our attention from the cosmos to the nature of man the old questions of nominalism and realism reappear. Summing up, we can say that the educational world has developed two major theories as a result of two quite different conceptions of human nature. One looks upon man simply as a chance product of nature itself which has produced at random plants, crocodiles, and men with no more interest in one than in the other. Nature itself is not a constant, in fact its most characteristic feature is change. Therefore it follows that there is nothing constant or permanent in man. He is just the end product of constantly changing forces and must constantly make readjustment to them. Finally he dies like the plant and the crocodile, and that is the end of the story. This theory has resulted in what is known as the progressive movement in education. It is a soft approach.

The other major theory looks upon human nature as a constant because it has within itself a spiritual entity which, while it may grow as it adjusts itself to the universal and unchanging, still retains its identity. This is the conception which has held sway for ages although it is not as fashionable as it was. If it does not include the totality of the Christian view of human nature, at least it is not at odds with it. The existence of Greatness which, at the same time, transcends and molds man is consonant with Christianity, and its educational method has some iron in it because, in the last analysis, its conception of human nature is immeasurably higher than that of its principal rival.

However, we find that there are many problems which cluster about these major points of view. Some of them cut across the main divisions of thought indicated above, helping to confuse the situation still further. One of them is the question of the freedom of the will. La Place, the philosopher, believed that freedom of the will is illusion. Every effect has an antecedent cause so that even the lightest word, the most flickering emotion, is the result of what has gone before. We have no more freedom than the billiard ball which moves only when it is struck with a cue. Our feelings, our thoughts, our actions were written in the stars (or the molecules) at the creation of the world. If all could be known by a supreme intelligence, the future of the world and of everyone in it could be predicted with complete accuracy. While modern science has disrupted the basis of this philosophy by showing that there are areas where chance seems to prevail, this theory has had its effect upon educational procedures. The behaviorists have subscribed to it and have endeavored to describe human nature by denaturing it, leaving out such concepts as consciousness, mind, purpose and will. Only the outer act can be described as good or ill because the inner state of the individual is as ungettable as the nature of the cosmos itself. It is unknowable even to the individual concerned because he is unaware of the antecedent forces of which he is the end product. Naturally, according to this belief, man is as irresponsible as the above mentioned billiard ball which moves only when it is pushed. Man is one with the inorganic world. He cannot act; he can only react.

The behaviorists have lost ground in the educational world but there are determinists of various sorts who put the emphasis on the outer environment rather than on the power of the individual to transcend or at least to choose his environment. The task of education, therefore, is to supply the proper milieu. There is here, as well as elsewhere in the variegated philosophy of the naturalists, an inconsistency because *someone* must be able to break out of this iron determinism and act freely in order to create conditions which will automatically bring about the right reaction in others. Of course, they might say that their determinism to do this was also written in the stars.

However, many educationists cannot go along with strict determinism. The progressives believe that in this changing and dynamic universe there is real freedom and genuine novelty.[3] They repudiate the notion that nothing can happen without an antecedent cause. The past to them does not contain or control all of the possibilities of the future. Therefore they say that the child is not only free to choose but that he has the right to choose. This may mean that the child may reject the instruction of the teacher and indicate what kind of instruction he

[3] It is only fair to the progressives to bring out that here they are in agreement, although on different grounds, with the Christian belief in a margin of freedom for the human will and in the possibility of miracle. The Christian emphatically does not subscribe to the theory that the past controls the present.

wants. This, to some, will seem like the *reductio ad absurdum;* but in actual practice the progressives carry their doctrine to the point of saying that the curriculum should be tailored to the class and not the class to the curriculum. Ideally, it should be custom made for each individual. The right to freedom of choice implies much about classroom method. The class no longer sits with folded hands at desks fixed to the floor in geometric patterns, outwardly quiet but inwardly rebellious. Seats are movable and the child can talk naturally to his neighbor and roam around the room if the fancy strikes him. One should seldom say "No" to a child since this abridges his freedom and does him some obscure psychic injury. In justice to the progressives this is not as absurd as it sounds; at least it can be stated that the fundamental idea is that the child is good and that, under expert guidance, his interest can be aroused so that he studies from desire and not from compulsion. Many of us of an older generation can remember the deadly dullness of many classrooms conducted under the old system. Maybe that was as bad as a classroom that seems like a shambles.

Another of the emergent problems is whether or not there can be a goal, a desired end, an objective universally valid toward which education should strive. Here, again, we see the division of opinion between the modern realists and the modern nominalists. The realists, believing that goodness, truth and beauty are universals having objective existence and the power to attract that which is universal in human nature, have less difficulty in describing such a goal than the nominalists. The goal of education, according to them, is to bring each individual into transforming contact with that which is universally true. As a matter of practice, it means exposing him to the funded experience of the race as it has shown its timeless value from age to age. The classics have endured throughout the centuries because of their intrinsic worth. Science as a method of exploring the physical universe has a perennial value. The educational realist does not believe that this involves jamming each pupil into a Procrustean bed which hinders his natural growth and breaks his intellectual spirit; rather, he thinks that this rich heritage, if properly taught, will inspire the pupil to creative activity. He will have the raw material without which it is impossible to think to any purpose. This approach is subject centered, to be sure, and does involve discipline and drudgery, but the self-mastery acquired is also a part of education. Out of this process alone will come maturity of character, judgment, the love of learning, and the spirit of scholarship. Such is the goal of the realist.

The nominalist, or progressive, takes a diametrically opposite point of view. Denying that there are absolutes in the cosmos and in the nature of man, this school holds that there is no end toward which either the individual or the universe moves. Therefore education can have no fixed goal. Education in this dynamic and changing world calls for a constant reconstruction of experience in terms of immediate problems and pressures. Ends are always proximate ends and change from day to day. The intelligent progressive would not say that the past experience of the race has no value even though he is such a pronounced believer in presentism. All that he would allow, however, is that if historical data can be used to solve immediate problems, it has a certain value. Instead of emphasizing mastery of a subject, he feels that knowledge should only be called on, here and there, for some instrumental purpose. Growth itself is the goal, and then more growth; no other goal can be set because the future is entirely unpredictable. It is only fair to say that the progressive is not consistent. Dewey, for example, is not consistent when he allows that the good society (which he identifies with democracy) should be kept in mind. At the same time, the true progressive, if pushed into a corner, would insist that education can have no fixed goals because the universe, as it blunders along, is not built that way.

There are also diverse opinions in the educational world about the nature of knowledge. By "knowledge" we mean not the acquisition of a mass of miscellaneous information of the sort that would enable one to shine in a quiz program, but knowledge in the sense of contact with reality or truth. The realist (please remember that we are using this term in the medieval sense—say "traditionalist or essentialist if you like) holds with what is called the "correspondence theory." This claims that we can pierce through to the inner meaning of the objective world—in other words that we can know the truth about it. Thus we may not understand all of the intricacies of a watch, but we do comprehend its essential "watchness" which is its ability to mark off the intervals of time. In a

sense we intuit its reality so that there is a direct correspondence between what the watch really is and our
knowledge. So, we may have an understanding of the
inner meaning and significance of the universe although
we may not comprehend all of the complexities of its
physical structure. What the teacher has to do is to impart this knowledge, and because it is a knowledge of the
truth, it is the duty of the pupil to assimilate it. He can
do so because human nature is *capax veritatis* even as it
is *capax Dei*. He may refuse to appropriate this truth;
but if he does so, it is the worse for him.

Many educators do not agree with the theory above
outlined. They hold that the "consistency theory" brings
us as near to truth as we shall ever get. This theory claims
that truth is always refracted by the human senses so that
what the mind receives cannot possibly square with
reality. An oar, half in the water, seems to be bent, and
this suggests that all of our sense impressions may be
"bent" in the same way. So these nominalists believe that
though there is an external world, an exact correspondence between our knowledge and the outer reality is out
of the question. The only thing on which we can rely is
the consistency between our observations under controlled conditions and those of the great majority of normal people. If these impressions coincide we may accept
the result as a sort of working, day-to-day truth.

The pragmatists do not bother even with the consistency theory and have been charged with being anti-intel-
lectuals. There is nothing high-flown or fancy about them
—no prying into ultimates. Truth or knowledge is sim-

ply what works now. Pragmatism gives the impression that truth is just an improvisation, a nostrum which leaves us uneasily conscious that we have taken the wrong medicine.

Mysticism, as a source of knowledge, is discarded by educators as a worthless tool. They have no use for what has been called the "sixth sense," through which man claims that he comes into contact with reality. The experience, whatever it is, is held to be ineffable and therefore sterile.

Revealed truth in the religious sense does not fare much better. The attitude of many educators toward it is antagonistic. The progressive must find it difficult, if not impossible, to square his fundamental attitude toward reality with that of the Church and I have a suspicion, though with no means of proving its accuracy, that the definite hostility to the Church which exists in certain parts of the educational world, has its origin in this group. Perhaps there may be the feeling that the separation of Church and State precludes the use of definitely religious ideas in secular educational theory. The common charge against revealed truth is that once accepted there is no further opportunity for argument. There is no doubt of the fact that this anti-religious approach has gained much ground in the educational world, and that this is not unconnected with the increasing secularism of the country. Educators like to feel that everything is open to question—that nothing is finally settled. Whatever the reason may be, secular educators do not look on revealed truth as a source of knowledge.

Not only are educators confused by what is meant by knowledge, they are also in disagreement about values. They are greatly concerned about values, however, because they realize that only in this field can they recapture unifying objectives. To state one's sense of values is to state one's aims.

Here, again, we must return to the fundamental question of the realist and the nominalist. The question is whether values are objective or subjective. Do values exist independently of man or are they an internal matter? The realist would claim that there are intrinsic values which are a part of the fundamental structure of the universe. The moral code expressed in the Decalogue is universally valid; it corresponds to reality and man may disregard it only at his peril. So, in the field of natural objects, a chair has intrinsic value because of its form and is there to be used although no one has the sense to sit in it. The universe, likewise, because its structure and form are filled with meaning and purpose, is a chair in which we may sit if we will. The intrinsic value (or form) of the cosmos undergirds and informs all particular and limited values.

Nominalists dispute this idea saying that value resides only in the mind of the individual who finds that certain things are of use to him. A book is valuable only because it is valued. Truth itself has no value except as it serves some useful purpose; only as it is used instrumentally does its value come into being. Hence children should study what they like because only what interests them has value so far as they are concerned. This theory, carried to the extreme, makes all values relative. This does not seem to bother many educators.

Common sense tells us that to value and to evaluate are two different things. What is desired may not be desirable; some authority must determine a scale of values. Educational realists endeavor to erect a rational scale of values saying that they should be chosen in harmony with cosmic design. Inclusive values should rank exclusive ones thus barring out selfish choices. The highest values are intrinsic and therefore the highest form of happiness is sheer intellectual contemplation.[4] However, this is hotly disputed by the nominalists who look askance at establishing a ladder of values. They feel that values should be established experimentally and should have the same tentative and provisional character as truth. A fixed scale cannot be determined in a world whose only constant is change and for this reason values will always fluctuate. This point of view is maddening to the realist when he thinks of the implications. Extermination camps seemed valuable to Hitler.

The National Education Association, giving up all hope of agreement on ultimate values and objectives, has been forced to offer what it regards as *proximate* ends in the form of immediate day-to-day objectives. They are as follows: health; command of fundamental processes

[4] Compare this thought with the Christian idea of worship as the supreme activity in which all of the faculties come to a focus in an act of contemplation.

with the "three Rs" as a basis; worthy home membership; vocation; civic functions; worthy use of leisure time; and ethical character.[5]

This is a confession of defeat. The best thinkers in the field of public education have endeavored to replace on a naturalistic basis the old metaphysic of the Church and they have failed. The individual teacher has a choice of at least half a dozen points of view about fundamental philosophy and as many about educational procedures. Ideally the teacher should be working under the aegis of a unified and purposeful philosophy. Ideally the pupil should progress from grade to grade without being subjected to, and confused by, the whims of successive teachers. Actually most teachers are bewildered and do the best they can from day to day.

It is impossible for anyone to consider the mental confusion together with the consequent limited, proximate, and sometimes trivial objectives of the public school world without asking himself whether or not something of supreme value was not lost when education was cut in two. Religion looks on life and ponders its significance from the standpoint of eternity. It believes that life, with its meaning, purpose, and vocation can only be lived well when it is recognized that the soul has an immortal, as well as a terrestrial, destiny. This sense that while man is in the time sequence, he still has that within him which transcends time is deep in the heart of the religious attitude.

The school system, taking it by and large, is com-

[5] See *Modern Philosophies of Education* by Brubacher, p. 110.

pletely immersed in time and in the affairs of the world. This is natural enough, for from the standpoint of naturalism, death is the end; the horizon both for the individual and the planet is severely limited. This shortened view diminishes man's belief in the dignity and the possibilities of human nature and profoundly influences the philosophies of education. With its conceptions untouched by intimations of destiny and grandeur, education tries as best it can to teach man to adjust to the limited circumference of his existence. Teach him to get along with his fellows; give him a trade so that he can earn a living; administer some mental pabulum if he can absorb it—mottoes like these are the inevitable deductions of any philosophy based on naturalism.

It would be false to intimate that there may not be a sort of pathetic nobility in naturalism. Some naturalists, like Herbert Spencer, attempt to deduce a code of morals by watching the results of cause and effect in human affairs. Others, like Nietzsche, from exactly the same premises, deduce a moral code which is repulsive to a man of any sensibility. As Hocking says:

It [naturalism] does not *necessarily* turn man back into a pigsty, nor reverse the direction of social advance. Only its ethos lacks the vistas of eternity and the resonance of divine concern in its inward vitality. It is man's gesture of heroism on the scaffold of a universe which will eventually write a cypher as the sum of all his works.[6] (Italics mine.)

[6] W. E. Hocking. *Types of Philosophy* (New York: Charles Scribner's Sons, 1929), p. 87. Used by permission.

CHAPTER 5

Truth Is Personal

Who hath measured the waters in the hollow of his hand, and meted out heaven with the span, and comprehended the dust of the earth in a measure, and weighed the mountains in scales, and the hills in a balance? Who hath directed the Spirit of the Lord, or being his counsellor hath taught him? . . . To whom then will ye liken God? or what likeness will ye compare unto him?—*Isaiah* 40:12-18.

And, Thou, Lord, in the beginning hast laid the foundation of the earth; and the heavens are the works of thine hands. They shall perish; but thou remainest; and they shall wax old as doth a garment; And as a vesture shalt thou fold them up, and they shall be changed: but thou art the same, and thy years shall not fail.—*Hebrews* 1:10-12.

Let not your heart be troubled: ye believe in God, believe also in me. In my Father's house are many mansions: if it were not so, I would have told you.—*John* 14:1-2.

Passages like these, chosen almost at random, used to be in the minds of educators before the separation of Church and State. They indicate the background structure of the universe as they conceived it and all that they taught was in harmony with its majestic proportions. God, the creator of all this wonder, was indescribably great, indescribably good, and from this contact with Greatness man derived his own dignity and significance.

From this great Other he derived also his essential security, and in him he had the hope of eternal life. Man was in his Father's house, and in that house were many mansions.

When one compares the nobility of this conception of reality with the pedestrian, commonplace, and diverse insights of secular philosophers, he is aware of what has been lost since secular education has been on its own. We no longer live in a house; we live in a shack based on the sand and open to every harsh and terrifying wind that blows. Modern education does not expose us to greatness, nor does it introduce us to humility. It likes to debunk. While we have been intrigued by the effort to destroy our illusions concerning individuals, we have not been aware that secular education, after having cast off its ancient moorings, is debunking the universe itself and human nature along with it. You and I have not escaped.

The Christian faith makes a sharp protest against this decline into impersonality. The Christian educator says that Truth has its essence in personality both divine and human, and that reality itself consists in the interplay of person and person. The only greatness is personal greatness, not the distances of interstellar space. The material universe, these bodies which we wear, are but the scaffolding of personality, and while we can deduce the laws of matter, these laws are but secondary and derivative aspects of truth. When the person is left out truth begins to shrink. When science begins to philosophize without the person, it is like the squeaking of bats in a dark cave. We are expected to look at some algebraic equation as if it contained the mystery of life. Science treats not only things as objects but men as objects, and that reduces man to the level of a thing. We may split the atom and pierce the galaxies, but we shall never know the inwardness of things save as the mantle of personality. They have no other meaning. To understand "inwardness," there must be the subject to subject relationship, the "I" encountering the "Thou" as Buber says. The truck driver knows this. He is not concerned with the inwardness of a chair, but he is concerned about his relationship with his wife, his union, his boss. Truth only climbs to full stature in personality. The philosopher leaves off his work at five o'clock and goes home for a good dinner and good company. He is immediately cured of his depression; his pale and dreary thoughts leave him the moment he touches something real. We only exist in relationships which are perpendicular toward God and horizontal toward men. This is why the Cross is such a powerful symbol of reality. All the real problems of life dwell in this region. All else is commentary.

However, it is probable that I have been unfair to the various schools of thought I have endeavored to describe in the preceding chapter. I should hasten to add that each one of them has got hold of *something,* a fragment, a piece without the whole, with no more relationship to its environment than a pair of roller skates in a jungle. On the level that these men have been thinking, there is no possibility of reconciling apparent opposites. A new dimension is necessary if paradoxes are to be resolved, and that can only be found in God, who is the master of paradox, who seems in fact to glory in paradox.

In God there is the reconciliation of the realist and the nominalist. God is the great Universal; as such all lesser universals draw their substance from his being and have objective reality. The one word big enough to be used in connection with the central universal is love. Yet love demands a particular object, else it would not be love. God loves each man in his particularity, but he also loves him because he has a universal element in him which corresponds to the universal in every other man. They are all sons and so can respond to the universal father. Christ, as perfect Son and also as perfect individual, is *the* concrete universal. The general and the particular do meet, and the general, or universal, is more than a mental convenience for the purposes of thought. They belong together, they presuppose each other, without them there would be neither general nor particular. In this necessary connection and, at the same time, tension between the two poles we have reality.

In the conception of Truth as personal, we have the reconciliation of the Absolute and the Changing. For a scientist, operating in his proper sphere, to claim that he has arrived at an absolute would mean an end of thinking and that would be absurd. The scholar, operating in his own area, can only come to tentative conclusions. No theory in the subject-object relationship can hope to be final for the foreseeable future. The Christian thinker must be as zealous for academic freedom as anybody else. But just as the Christian thinker has a different conception of ultimate truth from that of the scientist, so he has a different conception of the absolute. In terms of personality absolutes are possible. Nothing can be conceived beyond sacrificial and heroic love. Christ, hanging on the cross, is a symbol of this personal absolute because here God has revealed his innermost nature. We cannot think of anything beyond this; it is impossible to wish for anything beyond it. Of course, it is a bit strange to think in these terms. We are so accustomed to hem and haw in other regions. We almost admire the scholar's indecision and open mind; so much is this the case, that anything as decisive as the Absolute rather frightens us. Yet here we have it—*Finality*—and we find it in the person of Christ the image of the invisible God. Unlike the shallow conception of an algebraic formula, even granting that it allows for every phenomenon from the innermost recesses of the atom to the composition of the farthest star, this is an absolute in terms of personal quality. Yet it has unplumbed depths of meaning, for love may gradually reveal its scope and power in unsuspected areas of life here on earth and in the unimaginable encounters and relationships of the life to come. Love has its heights, its depths, its unsearchable riches; yet here and hereafter it is always love, the same yesterday, today, and forever. We can plunge into this absolute which eternally retains its universal character while dealing in myriad ways with its various objects.

Here is the answer to man's longing for the changeless, for that which cannot be shaken. He can abide change, the unexpected development, the onslaught of circumstance, the shock of bereavement provided that he may still feel that he is in touch with the love of God. In that "absolute" he has the peace that passes understanding. Yet the Christian thinker recognizes change as an essential element in reality. No one note, without giving way to others, can produce a melody. The Christian grows alert (in the best progressive manner) as he solves each problem that presents itself. While he breasts the wave, however, it is not in the spirit of one whose head is bloody but unbowed; he does not thank whatever gods there be for his unconquerable soul, nor blow the trumpet, like Childe Roland, in the midst of brooding menace. Such pride is not for him as he proceeds on his way tranquilly and humbly under the guidance of another star. In him the absolute and the changing are reconciled.

The Christian conception of Truth provides the only possible reconciliation of determinism and free will. In Christian thought there is a firm grasp of the reality of determinism but this is based not on the accidental collocations of atoms at the time of creation, but on the determining characteristics of love. God's love is not just an easy-going good nature; it is more than a vast amiability. Rather, it is jealous, possessive, full of fire, impregnated with purpose for his creation and for each man's life. If this were not so, it would be puzzling to hear Christ say, "My meat is to do the will of him that sent me," and declare that his true relatives are those who likewise are seeking to do God's will for them. It is not hard to believe in some vast impersonal force; such a be-

lief takes little intellectual grasp and certainly demands
no moral effort. It is difficult to believe that God sent his
Son, born of a woman in Bethlehem of Judea, to redeem
the world. This is the *scandal of singularity* of which
Casserley speaks.[1] It is also hard to believe that God
knows each man by name, numbers the hairs of his head,
is aware of his going out and his coming in, and, above
all, that he has a plan for each man's life which dovetails
into the great plan of creation. Here again is the scandal
of singularity; the Christian definitely believes that the
love of Christ constrains him. Here is determinism, but it
is the determinism of love and it can be denied. Man can
say "No." Because the power of choice remains, this determinism is completely at odds with the determinism of
a Bertrand Russell which admits of no choice whatever.
In a magnificent passage Russell writes:

That man is the product of causes which had no prevision of
the end they were achieving; that his origin, his growth, his
hopes and fears, his loves and beliefs are but the outcome of
accidental collocations of atoms; that no fire, no heroism, no
intensity of thought can preserve the individual's life beyond
the grave; that all the labors of the ages, all the devotion, all
the inspiration, all the noonday brightness of human genius
are destined to extinction in the vast death of the solar system
and that the whole temple of man's achievement must in-
evitably be buried beneath the debris of a universe in ruins—
all these things, if not quite beyond dispute, are yet so nearly

[1] For a discussion of this "scandal" read J. V. L. Casserley's
The Christian in Philosophy (London: Faber and Faber, Ltd.:
1949).

certain that no philosophy which rejects them can hope to stand.[2]

Here is realism indeed, and we admire the courage of the man who wrote such words—although, as Lecomte du Nouy says, it is curious to see a man arguing with such set purpose to prove that no such thing as purpose exists.

The Christian, however, has his moments of realism too; he also looks facts in the face and says in even more august language that "the heavens shall wax old as doth a garment"—but he adds that God is the same and that his years shall not fail. At the bottom of all this discussion about free will and determinism is the profound thought that it is God who has made us and not we ourselves; for this reason we yield a glad and willing obedience. "Our wills are ours to make them thine." The instinct for obedience which lurks in every heart and is a corollary to the instinct for self expression (strange that the progressives do not see this) stems from this unconscious acceptance of God as creator and sovereign. The true soldier rejoices that he is under authority. The boy likes the leader who has that something which makes him jump to obey. Children like the teacher who keeps command of the classroom, and the well earned rebuke strikes a responsive chord. All this has its theological connotations about the nature of man who in his heart makes a willing response to greatness.

[2] Quote from *The Road to Reason* by Lecomte du Nouy (Toronto: Longmans, Green and Co., 1955) p. 191. Used by permission.

Yet the other side to obedience is the fact that in submission to this kind of determinism man is obeying a Love which is infinitely concerned about his welfare and development. God knows us better than we know ourselves and directs us in the path which leads to the fullest self-realization. Through the courtesy of Love its whisper to our hearts can scarcely be distinguished from the voice of our best selves. The touch of God adds to our stature. Humility is the foundation of greatness.

Truth as personal solves the ultimate questions of knowledge. Of all the theories of knowledge evolved by the philosophic mind the "correspondence theory" appeals to the Christian thinker because it allows man the intuitive power to grasp the intangible real. So the Christian, learned or unlearned, may not understand the complexities of the material universe, but he does comprehend its essence as the garment of God. The shepherds at the Christmas manger knew as much about what was going on as the wise men. The wise men saw the star, but the shepherds heard the songs of the angels—on the whole a more inspiring role, for (don't forget) reality is personal. Yet the men of science had their place at the manger even though, in the deepest sense, they did not *know* any more than the shepherds. So the Christian welcomes the researches of science and does not fear fact as fact, believing that every fact, when seen in its full relationship with other facts, bears witness to the glory of God. Unfortunately, the Church has failed to keep abreast of research, and so interpretation has lagged behind discovery.

It is hard to be patient with the "consistency theory" of knowledge when it ceases to be a description of a scientific method and tells us that, as in the analogy of the oar "bent" in the water, we can have only a bent conception of the universe. It is true that the light of the sun, the sparkle on the water, the blue of the sky, the music of the violin, the warmth of the fire—all in fact that makes life human and livable can be dissolved by analysis into something impersonal and inhuman. But we are told that these vibrations, photons, or what not, are the real thing even though we cannot perceive them. This theory, when it attempts to philosophize, tells us that we can have no confidence in the evidence of our own senses. Where this line of reasoning would end if followed to a logical conclusion is not disclosed, but it is really all rather dreadful when we stop to think, dreadful if it were not so ridiculous. If light is not light, sound not sound, nor color color, then love is not love, for it along with all other human experiences suffers from this same refraction. Gone would be the relationship of family and friends; gone, along with love, would be the sense of duty and of aspiration. All would be "bent." This, of course, is the veriest nonsense. It is true that we help to create this universe of light and color and of love as we react to that which is without. Every moment of our lives is a miracle of creation. But color is color, sound is sound, and the rustle of the wind in the trees, and the call of the birds, and the thunder of the surf, and the whisper of love are what they seem. If this were not so, we might well be terrified by the unknown "real" out there—conceiving that we are but points of light in a surrounding and terrifying darkness. It is strange how people will swallow such a philosophy but will boggle at the fact that God so loved the world that he gave his only begotten Son.

The Church agrees with the pragmatist that truth must work, and it claims that the majestic truth of Revelation works and has an instrumental value never equalled by any naturalistic philosophy. But the Church profoundly disagrees with the pragmatist in making truth of such puny, transitory, and changing dimensions. Both the consistency and pragmatist theories are letdowns from the truth contained in the great verses with which this chapter opened, and in this deterioration the dignity of man disappears. The descent is into the subhuman.

We have seen how much confusion exists in the educational world about values and, therefore, objectives. The realist (or essentialist) claims that there are universal values which are valid for every man. These values, having their being in the structure of the universe, should be arranged in harmony with cosmic design. The nominalist (or romantic progressive) believes that value is subjective—that it exists only in the mind of the valuer. Value, therefore, is measured by interest. The Church, as may be expected, in this as well as other matters, is on the side of the realist. Goodness, truth, and beauty are a part of the character of God. "Why callest thou me good?" Jesus asked. "There is no one good but God."

Our goodness is something which we breathe in like

the ozone which is already there as a gift from God. Our
sense of purpose is real because it is something caught
from a central purpose. Our virtue, intelligence, sense of
beauty, fineness of feeling are absorbed from a central
source. We love because he first loved us—yet by a miracle or paradox these values are ours as well. Value is one
with God which means that it is the same for every man.
It does not vary as men of different ages, races, and cul-
tures evoke it from their own nervous systems or from
the environment. Value is not an entity which can be cut
up and separated from value everywhere. It is like gravi-
tation, which is the same here and millions of light years
away. Through pain and loss and strife men press on
toward the intrinsic values of the universe. Men are reborn in every age and in every race, and when this happens, value begins to assume the same dimensions in the
most diverse minds.

From the standpoint of educational philosophy this
means that certain things have universal validity. In a
very real sense the curriculum should not be tailored to
the children; they should be tailored to the curriculum.
I guess this is what St. Paul had in mind when he said,
"Let God be true though every man be false." Unless this
is so, the hope that some day the brotherhood of man will
be realized is a vain one.

Yet, in the kingdom of God, values are subjective as
well as objective—indeed, it is hard to separate the two.
When God touches the soul, it is as if an electric switch
had lighted up an entire landscape with many prospects
begging for attention. Interest is born because one sees

himself a co-worker in an exceedingly exciting enterprise. With interest comes the sense that the kingdom of God, in all of its numberless manifestations, is the most valuable thing in the world. The whole question is rather silly. Objective and subjective cannot get along without each other. The danger is that we shall become interested in something which does not merit our attention or call forth our best powers.

Human nature is good only in the sense that even in the most depraved there is an essential sonship which can arise and go to the Father. By paradox, and in keeping with a religion which is alive with paradoxes, the conception is at once much lower and at the same time infinitely higher than that of the romantic progressives. Man's heart is a battle ground and his instincts are *not* all good. Yet he has a margin of free will which is both the condition of his manhood and at the same time the Achilles heel of his individuality. By the wrong use of it he can cut himself loose from the Source of all good and gradually become in the strictest sense of the word, a lost soul. The essence of this condition is that alienation from God which the Church calls sin. Man is powerless of himself to help himself, but the grace of God can turn the stubborn will or strengthen the weak knees. In Christ, God the Son died for each man in some mysterious manner clearing the way for a return. The atonement is real though it is hard to explain, even to understand. Something happened, a transaction of some sort. We can feel it with the heart better than explain it with the mind. Words are not deep or powerful enough to show all that was involved in this supreme act of search. "We only know he hung and suffered there." Here is the Truth seeking for us. Christ still lives, The Man, The Person of universal history, through whom all things were made, in whom all things consist, seeking for individual men and women, boys and girls. Sacrificial love like this can win men when it is interpreted by the saints of the Cross, both clerical and lay—sometimes, I think, especially lay. Men can arise, they can be reborn. Even though they have not attained, yet through repentance and faith they have a foothold. Their glance is toward the light, and their only plea at the day of judgment is that they have looked and are looking toward Jesus, the author and finisher of their faith. They have not attained, but they "press toward the mark for the prize of the high calling of God in Christ Jesus."

These are not the proximate and limited aims of modern educational theory. They are the ultimate ends which satisfy the deepest instincts of the human heart.

CHAPTER 6

Reclaiming Its Own Curriculum

While one can make a good case for the Christian religion as the only means of introducing significance, unity, and purpose into the entire educational process, it is not so simple to show how this is to be done. The American public would, I think, be shocked if it comprehended what the dominant educational philosophy really is and how far school thinking has departed from the faith of the people. They would be shocked, but they would not be prepared to tell the Church what to do about it. The public school officials, even though they may be devoted Christians, are not turning to the Church for any solution of their problems; and if they did, the Church would not have any ready answers. It must be confessed that only here and there is the Church even conscious of the problem for it has not yet learned to think of education, both secular and religious, as an indivisible unit—a seamless robe. There is, in fact, little informed opinion on either side. Most of the thinking about the relation of the Christian Church and its faith to the school world has been on the college level, and one can secure a good many books on the subject if he cares to do so. In this book we are dealing with the first twelve grades as being most critical in the life of youth from the educational standpoint. We believe that there are battles to be fought before the boy and girl go through the college gates, if indeed, they get that far at all; and that if they are not decided at an earlier age, it will be touch and go as to what happens later. In these pre-college years we have unexplored territory and in it we can see three educational forces at work. There are the full time private schools under Church and other auspices. Their limited number bears no relationship to the importance of their contribution. Their place in the educational scheme of America will be discussed in a later chapter. There are also, of course, the public schools and, for want of a better term, the Sunday schools. The Sunday school may have a week day session with or without the cooperation of the public school authorities—in any case I refer to the effort of individual churches throughout the country to erect a system of religious instruction. The public schools, in all probability, are here to stay. They rest on the sound theological basis that God has made of one blood all nations of men and we believe in the public schools in spite of all the rough things we have said about them. The Church, which likewise has many and grievous faults, is also here to stay. The problem is how to achieve a fruitful relationship between these powerful forces instead of the no-relationship which exists at present.

The Church may expect no overtures from the public schools for a good many reasons; among them is the fact that most school people look upon the Church's educational efforts with good-natured contempt. The Church may just as well be realistic and admit that this attitude is, to a great extent, justified, although historically it is easy enough to see how it all came about. When, in the early days of our country's history, the Church surrendered its responsibility to the State, education was still in its elementary stages. If the boys and girls mastered their "three Rs," there was nothing particularly alarming about that. This slight increase in literacy was not enough to inspire the Church to re-examine its educational procedures at the time. The Episcopal Church, for example, saw no reason to feel that the Prayer Book injunction to teach the ancient catechism did not cover the requirements of religious education very well indeed. The life of the community still centered around the Church; the parson was still the best educated man in it and his opinions carried great weight. There were no daily newspapers, and people were not exposed to every wind of doctrine both religious and political. The children were not taught subjects in school which might upset religious convictions, and these convictions, moreover, were a part of the very atmosphere they breathed. The catechetical theory was a sound one for the time; it was not sound as years and generations passed, and secular influences and philosophies began to play upon the youthful mind.

In spite of all this the Church hung on to its medieval conception of education though the conditions which had given rise to it no longer existed. There were a few twinges of conscience, and Sunday schools taught by lay people began to come into existence about the middle of the last century, or perhaps a few years earlier, but they seemed so unimportant that for a time the clergy had nothing to do with them. Their attitude was aided and abetted by the theological seminaries which, until very recent years, have acted as if the Sunday schools were hardly worth their attention. Later on, various groups began to publish Sunday school materials, but the whole effort was completely insulated from the public schools and no attempts were made to learn about educational techniques which the public schools were finding valuable. It was a rather pathetic fumbling in the dark, and for generations the Sunday school was a sort of parish orphan. Only lately has the Church realized that changed conditions demand a revolution in its attitude and method. Better textbooks are being published, many parishes are erecting educational buildings with private classrooms, and a start is being made in training lay people to teach more effectively. This is all of great significance, but the handicap of a hundred years in which the Church did not think in educational terms cannot be overcome in a year or so. While we may regret it, we can understand why the Church cannot, at the moment, face the great world of public school education with an informed opinion, both professional and lay, which the secular educationists would consider worthy of attention.

The first step of the Church toward helping to put the whole educational house in order is obviously to redouble its efforts to put its own house in order. It must perform better the limited role to which by general agreement it has been assigned, before it can assume a larger part. If the Church does not really come to its senses from an educational point of view in the comparatively near future, even that small part will be taken away. It is still as true as when the words were first spoken that "to him that hath shall be given and that from him that hath not shall be taken away even that which he hath." It should be realized that the mammoth school bureaucracy (the biggest in the United States) can easily and almost by accident destroy the educational system of the Church, or at least render it so innocuous that it will not be worthy of sympathy or support. It is as clear as crystal to anyone who studies the situation, that, unconsciously for the most part, the public school system is making an assault on religious education.

I say "unconsciously for the most part" because there are spots in the educational field which are definitely hostile to the Church and all that it stands for. These men are in teachers' colleges, in administration, and in the classroom. They feel that the Church is a nuisance, and that any attempt at cooperation ends in pure frustration. One does not hear much about this, for it is not politic to make a public stand against the Church, but the antagonism is there. These people have their own church—the Public School—and they believe that through the public school alone is to come salvation. The school, they say, is equal to any demand; it can replace Church and home; it is the new messiah. Back of all this is the lust for power, the desire to dominate. It is not strange that this segment of the school world is both jealous and fearful of this anachronism, the Church, which presumes to say that it, too, has a responsibility toward childhood and youth.

But other educators—and there are many such who harbor no violent antagonisms—are powerless to lessen a built-in struggle between an awakened Church, representing the nation on its religious side, and the public schools, representing the nation on its secular side. The public schools cannot help but undermine the influence of the Sunday school not only because of the unlimited demands they make on the pupils' time, but also, and principally, because they are possessed of a different spirit. Under the influence of the prevailing naturalistic philosophy which banishes God, scorns the idea of eternal life and has, in consequence, a sharply reduced estimate of human nature, the schools have no recourse but to adopt the prevailing standards of the world. Adjustment, conformity (itself an enemy of original thinking), skill enough to make a living (and a blessing on you if you get rich)—such tame ideals are inevitable once faith in human significance and eternal destiny have been abandoned. There can be no easy accord between the Church and an institution which has at its heart such a philosophy of disillusionment. The schools are dominated by a heresy and there can be no reconciliation until the issues are brought into the open and considered by the American public. The situation cannot be covered up forever for the Church has a responsibility to the nation which it must some time face. We shudder at the thought of a State Church. We may shudder at what we already have—a vast institution dominated by a heresy which the conscience of the country rejects and yet having the taxing and police power of the State in its possession.

As was stated at the beginning of this chapter, it is one thing to see the issues; it is another to know how to meet them. The Church, suffering from a century of mental apathy, will certainly accomplish nothing by firing broadsides at the public schools. To be brutally frank, it does not know enough about education to be able to do so effectively. Public school people have been thinking about education for generations, and they can talk us down with very little trouble. Moreover, they are our friends and neighbors—thoroughly good and nice people who are probably teaching our children five days in the week. But they are a part of a great system which has gradually evolved and for which no one person or group is responsible unless one wants to indict the entire American people. The Church may be right about some of the underlying issues (we think that it is), but it is not prepared to wage battle. What we can do is to look first to our own back yard and see how good a job we are doing in an area which is, by common consent, our own.

Any good schoolman can say to us, "You are finding fault with what we are doing. Let us ask you a few pertinent questions and let your conscience make the reply. How well are you transmitting to youth the vital inner experience of the Church? Are you making them see what real discipleship entails? Are they taking advantage of the spiritual resources in worship, sacrament, and study which the Church possesses? Are you awakening their minds by a knowledge of the great Judaeo-Christian tradition? In it you have one of the streams of human history, the greatest of the humanities telling the story of a remarkable people, rich with the biographies of great men and women, including that of the greatest man who ever lived, and all expressed in superb literary and poetic form. How well are you passing this on? We leave it all to you and it might well tax all of your powers. Why do you not begin to do this well before you come to us with your criticisms?"

There is not much that we can say to this hypothetical schoolman, for he hits us in a weak spot. We must realize that we are just beginning to catch a glimpse of the dimensions of our educational task. We must produce a teaching *order* of volunteer men and women who feel called to make teaching their avocation—truer to say, perhaps, their real mission in life. These men and women must learn about the problems of youth so that they can relate the Gospel to youthful needs; they must also become proficient in biblical content, exegesis, and higher criticism. They must know their Church and its history, know it well enough to earn the respect of public school people and scholars. When we have a group of such people in each church, we shall be in a position to answer such questions as the above and to meet the great army of the public school world with a friendly but determined army of our own.

We have come a certain way in our argument. Probably everyone will agree that we can make no mistake in endeavoring to hoe our own garden better. We may even be a little enthused to learn that in all this pother and bother about the humanities, our task is important for the Judaeo-Christian tradition overtowers them all. If we can keep this central humanity from going down the drain, it may be the means of preserving other hard-pressed classics as well. We may find, as we rise to our task, that the Church is the steward of more than one racial memory as well as of fundamental human rights.

But has the Church the right to allow itself to be confined strictly to the Judaeo-Christian tradition? To understand that tradition fully, one has to know something of general history. The Church of Israel was profoundly affected by the nations round about, and the Christian Church cannot be understood apart from the entire history of Europe and to a lesser extent of Asia. We cannot know the tradition simply as a system of thought—we must know it as it has been historically embodied and in vital contact with its times. It is difficult indeed to say just where the Christian study of history should stop for universal history is its background. To understand the tradition, then, no particular limit can be placed on its historical setting. Its adventures and its vicissitudes are a part of itself. Valley Forge reveals more about Washington than his speeches.

Another reason, too, may be given for this proposed enlargement of its curriculum by the Church—namely, that history is not well taught in the first twelve grades whatever may be its fate on the college level. There are dedicated teachers of history in the public schools, of course; but an attempt has been made to describe their handicaps in the chapter on academic freedom. It is hard to escape the conclusion of that chapter that the history textbooks in public school use have been so pared down, so robbed of life, that the teacher is hardly dealing with history at all or, at most, with a pale and ghostlike reflection of it. History should be taught straight from the shoulder, boldly, without attempting to evade unpleasant truths or to whitewash unpleasant episodes. Anything so full of life and passion as history should be taught with life and passion, not fearfully and timorously. To be sure, the teaching of history by the Church should be with God in the background as the great original, the great historic *fact* if you like, but that does not mean a slanted presentation of the human story. Interpretation is a different matter and the purpose of the Church should be to trace the providence of God through historic events.

Here, indeed, is a problem big enough to stir the spiritual and intellectual muscles of both teacher and pupil. There is a growing literature on the subject—*Christianity and History* by Herbert Butterfield is an excellent example. No easy answer can be found, yet this is *the* background problem of our times: is there *meaning* in the long and ofttimes tragic history of mankind? The Church of late years has left the interpretation of history in terms of God to certain fundamentalist sects who rely on an ancient method of biblical exegesis. Perhaps the Church has been afraid—who knows? Perhaps the prophetic sword has looked too heavy and sharp for its weak hand. But it could not once begin to teach universal history without having the question loom into sight around the first corner. Here would come a mental challenge—a specimen of what it would meet on every side the moment it leaves its closely guarded areas and gets down into the blood and sand of the arena. Of course, it would be partisan teaching if belief in God may be said to be partisan. The trouble with the teaching of history in the schools is precisely that it is *not* partisan. It is neutral teaching which fails of necessity to provoke mental activity. Hence we conclude that the Church must teach history: first, because it is an essential part of its own tradition; second, because it is not being taught well elsewhere; and, most of all, because it is an essential discipline in the quest of meaning in human life.

Neither can the Church continue to abandon the study of literature. Of course, in the Scriptures and the Apocrypha it has a beautiful chance to study literary appreciation and even to get in a good word for the study of Greek. But who will tell the Church that it should not follow this up by showing what her treasures in literature and poetry have been through the ages? The Scriptures have been the inspiration, the mother of great literature from the beginning, and it is the duty of the Church to see to it that its own classics become a common mental and spiritual possession of its people. This point was brought out forcibly in an address by Professor Jacques Maritain, at a seminar held at Kent School in which he made the following statement:

Coming now to education and our problem of Christian culture in the curriculum, I would say that in my opinion what is demanded is to get rid of those absurd prejudices which can be traced back to the Renaissance and which banish from the blessed land of educational curricula a number of authors and matters under the pretext that they are specifically religious and, therefore, not "classical" though they matter essentially to the common treasury of culture. The writings of the Fathers of the Church are an integral part of the humanities as well as, or more than, those of the Elizabethan dramatists; St. Augustine and Pascal matter to us no less than Lucretius or Marcus Aurelius. It is important for young people to know the history of astronomy or the history of Greek and Latin literature, but it is at least as important for them to know the history of the great theological controversies and the history of those works about spiritual life and mystical experience which have been for centuries jewels of Christian literature.[1]

There they lie, neglected on the library shelves: the Fathers, Origen, Tertullian, Augustine, the great mystics, St. Thomas Aquinas, and others too numerous to mention. This is obvious enough though little is done about it, for if the Church does not have these classics in its curriculum, who will? Are these treasures to be reserved for students in our seminaries, who, for the most part, are so busy reading their Bibles for the first time that they can only glance at the literature which lies just outside the Bible? Is this an esoteric knowledge? Is Christianity to become a mystery religion with its priests nodding sagely at each other about some hidden gnosis? Perish the thought. This material is for all.

However, it is also the duty of the Church to make its

[1] *The Christian Idea of Education,* edited by Edmund Fuller (New Haven: Yale University Press, 1957), p. 178. Used by permission.

people acquainted with the classics which are taught in the schools—with Milton, Thackeray, Tennyson, Browning, Melville, Hawthorne, T. S. Eliot, to mention only a few. A dreadful pall lies heavy over literature as well as over history. The lack of academic freedom is deadening, for such classics cannot be taught well without bringing out the Christian meaning and inspiration of the author. Innumerable other books lose their potency and charm when presented with only half an interpretation. Too many teachers are literary technicians and drive our students to drug store libraries. By way of parenthesis, it is mind jarring to think of the digested, reduced, or shall I say *mutilated*, books of permanent worth which are produced for high school use. The last one to come to my attention is *Moby Dick*, which has been reduced by a publishing company to the status of a poor "Western" because, forsooth, young people could not be expected to understand the religious and philosophical element which gives the book its real value.

It is perfectly evident that our high schools are not inculcating the love of good reading or any sense of discrimination. This is reflected by the kind of books which serve as mental pabulum for our people—many of them best sellers—whose obscenity is only eclipsed by the philosophy of life which peeps out here and there or is openly espoused by characters whom we are bidden to admire. Our people are reading books which are fit only for the ash can, and they do so without batting an eyelash. They seem to have no inward monitor, no standard of judgment which tells them that a certain book is trash.

The Roman Church is fully alive to this problem and publishes its Index. This is not the way of the non-Roman Church, but it has an equal duty to create an interior index which will be a guide to what is good and what is worthless. The public schools are not doing it. By every standard and test, therefore, the Church should resume the teaching of literature.[2]

The Church should teach philosophy and at the high school level. Its people should be aware of the impact made upon the philosophic mind of Europe by the Christian faith. The systems of Augustine should be familiar in their elements, while attention should be paid to such men as Kant, Spinoza, Berkeley, Hume, Hegel, Locke, and others. Our people should know the fundamental thought of Bertrand Russell and of the other naturalistic philosophers of the present day and attain a balance by a study of men like Hocking and Tillich of Harvard and Casserley of Seabury-Western Seminary.

High school students are fully capable, at least by the eleventh and twelfth grades, of studying philosophy. That it is not too far advanced for this age is indicated by the fact that there is talk of making it a regular high school

[2] Two books dealing with the Christian and Literature have recently appeared and are well worth reading. They are *American Literature and Christian Doctrine* by Randall Stewart (Baton Rouge: Louisiana State University Press, 1958) and *Man in Modern Fiction* by Edmund Fuller (New York: Random House, 1958). Mr. Stewart gives an analysis of Christian thought, or the lack of it, in the works of Melville, Hawthorne, Emerson and others; Mr. Fuller dissects the modern novel with a skillful and deft knife.

subject in the public schools. If this is the case, it is all the more necessary that the Church should teach it, for philosophy is high potency stuff. We want thinkers and philosophy makes people think, but some knowledge of it is also a necessary part of the Christian equipment. Our people must be able to see through the cheap and shallow philosophies, bastard offspring of legitimate science, which clutter up the modern stage. One meets shreds and patches of it everywhere. Many modern authors are followers of some type of naturalism which is a species of nature worship; these are the modern sophists who make the worse appear the better reason. Or they may be the modern worshippers of Baal and his fertility rites. Whatever they may be they are at one in dismissing God from his throne and in debunking man. It is necessary that our people should be able to recognize types and to know how they can be met and discomfited on their own ground. We must remember that the attack on Christianity is an intellectual one and that this kind of an attack can only be met by an intellectual defense.

The Great Tradition must have a bodyguard. That bodyguard consists of history, literature, and philosophy —and these the Church should teach. It must reclaim its own curriculum.

Author's Note:

Of course the public schools will continue to teach English and history. However, in teaching English, the author is in agreement with Dr. Conant's recommendation (page 50 in *The American High School Today*) that half of the time of the pupil in this subject should be devoted to English composition. English literature as well as history will still be taught, but the teachers of both will be handicapped by the limitations which are inherent in the public school system itself.

CHAPTER 7

Present Imperatives

The next step forward in the recapture of meaning is perhaps the simplest and, at the same time, the most difficult. Responsible as it is for man's retention of meaning, greatness, and destiny, it is for the Church to recover the sense of its own grandeur and significance. It is faced with the perennial problem of living up to its role.

Individuals have the same trouble. More men underestimate than overestimate themselves. When faced with a sudden challenge, they shrink because their conception of their own part in the drama has been a humdrum one. They are frightened by the possibility of playing a larger part. Unaware of their own capacities under stress, shrinking from new insights, they hesitate about big decisions and shy away from ventures into the unknown. They settle for the mediocre, fearful of the distant rolling drums. They fear meaning. This drag toward the meaningless in personal life is insidious—just as the pull toward the meaningful is disconcerting.

So the Church shrinks from its inherent responsibility for the whole of education in the deep sense of the word. It falters before its destiny, even though it may be uneasily conscious of its power. I say, therefore, that the first great difficulty is in the inner spirit rather than in any outer obstacle. Once the Church sees that in order to fulfill its own mission toward youth, it must come to grips with the total educational process, things can begin to happen immediately. As a matter of fact they *are* beginning to happen—harbingers, I hope, of greater things to come.

For one thing it must be fully recognized, as mentioned in the first chapter, that a great change has come over the Church in its attitude toward its educational responsibility. This is of the utmost significance, even though the full outlines of the task still remain indistinct. In the Episcopal Church, with which I am most familiar, the turn of the tide has been almost revolutionary. Its National Department of Christian Education is now given a dignified position in the total budget. It has expert leadership and its activities have been manifold. Its most obvious activity has been in the creation of a new series of textbooks for the church school curriculum. These are built on the theory that young people, as well as old, are capable of having religious experience and that religion can be of help in meeting their own very real problems. This, in itself, is a revolution. Youth has been consistently underestimated, both intellectually and spiritually, with the result that there has been an obscure notion—for church school objectives have not been clearly thought through—that young people were being prepared for something which was to happen later. Religion has been considered an adult enterprise. Biblical passages have been examined and moral lessons have been drawn, but the whole process simply has not worked. A generation has been produced that neither knows the Bible nor has had that early experience of the power of the Holy Spirit to guide, counsel, and to give inner strength. This abysmal ignorance of the Scriptures, the Church, and the experience of the living Christ was brought out dramatically during the war. In other directions it has been different. We send our boys and girls to summer camps, hoping for definite results. In more difficult cases we expect the psychiatrist to help. But up until recently people have sent their children to church school because it seemed like the decent and respectable thing to do, but not because they thought that much would happen to them as a result. Now it is different. We expect results in character and conduct. These young people are *capable* of religion and respond when the right approach is made. This new recognition of and respect for youth has already produced results.

Many would be astonished by the great number of young people in the Church who have grasped what the Christian religion is all about. These youngsters are active in their own parishes and are to be seen at great youth conferences, keen, devoted, eager to be of service, and demanding greater responsibilities. These are the ones who make the task of the public school teacher not only bearable but a joy, because they are eager, interested, purposeful, and possess an inner discipline which springs from a deep source. Here we see the connection between the Church's contribution in imparting meaning and zest at an early age and one of the great public school problems. These boys and girls go to school with an attitude and an aptitude the secret of which does not lie within the public school system itself. No law is violated. No fanatic can make objection, but the relationship between the Church and State effort is close indeed.

At the same time the national department of the Episcopal Church has emphasized what has been called the "Family Service." The spread of this custom over the entire nation has been one of the unnoticed miracles of modern times. Not alone in the realm of science do wonders take place, although these are the ones that get the headlines. Here we have evidence of a movement of the Spirit in the hearts of our people. Families go to church together. The old custom of having "opening exercises," or even more formal Sunday school worship services, is giving way to the family pew. When we stop to think of it, the idea that children and even young people should be required to create their own "atmosphere" seems ridiculous. It is like making them eat in the kitchen. To inculcate patriotism it is not enough to have a salute to the flag in the classroom. Young people must attend a patriotic rally and catch the spirit of the whole group. They must feel the impact of something intangible from their elders if they would recognize Greatness passing by. So youth must worship with age as it has done through the centuries; and this is precisely what is happening in thousands of churches throughout our land. Children worship in the family group, and both from the atmosphere of corporate devotion and from the example of their parents indelible impressions are made.

Another sign of the way the wind is blowing is in the new emphasis on teacher training. It is recognized that good teaching is a "Must" if observable results are to be obtained. The national department, diocesan authorities, and local clergy are paying more attention to this problem than ever before. In the theological seminaries there is a response to the new climate of public opinion and a striving to make their graduates educators as well as priests, pastors, and preachers. This is certainly a harbinger of the time when a lay teaching order in the Church will come into being. Teaching is an apostolic office and corresponds to a classic call of the Holy Spirit.

A part of the grandeur of the Church lies in its reserve power to create teachers who will offer themselves gladly for rigorous training and thus swell the ranks of another order of the ministry. I am referring now to volunteers, men and women of various occupations, who will make teaching their avocation. The greater the challenge, the greater the response will be. Teaching in church school and in its weekday session is coming to be seen as a glorious chance to serve God. The old conception of the Sunday school teacher as a person of good will, but with a hazy (*very* hazy) knowledge of the subject and a still dimmer idea of how to handle spirited youngsters, is giving way to a new image in the public mind. That image has more definite, and much more compelling, outlines. It envisages an alert and competent person, who, having given time and energy to an arduous preparation, can both instruct and, at the same time, evoke an inner response. Here is the sort of teacher who elicits the secret admiration of young minds and thus conveys soundless messages of insight and aspiration. The Church is great because it carries in its mighty heart the history of countless laymen and laywomen down through the ages who have consecrated themselves to a task and thus have found self-realization and freedom in the service of God. To think that the Church does not have within it the power to evoke such a response is to fail to realize its past history and its potential power. All that is needed is a vision of the enormous validity and productiveness of the teacher's job; then requisite leadership at all levels will be sure to come.

In addition to this, we see at the present time more and more young people who are training for full-time salaried positions in religious education. The professional is needed to guide the volunteer and to perform the background work of administration.

The leaders of my own Church (and all this can be matched in other communions) have led along another direction. They have seen that *only a converted parish can touch the heart of youth*. Real education is only partially the result of the classroom; it also comes when one feels the Spirit working through the Body. One might digress long enough, while on this matter of what may be called *incidental* education, to observe that this powerful movement of mass suggestion is not confined to the Church. What happens on the street corner, or in front of the drug store as a crowd loiters, may have a mighty effect. Sometimes we seem to steel ourselves to resist the attack direct, even when it is for our own good; but when the guard is down, things slip into our inmost souls—both good and bad things. The spirit of the town, as evinced by its responsible and irresponsible citizens, hits youth with the power of a sledge hammer. The standards, the conversation of the home, may help *or* undo all that may be said in class. But the Church has an unequalled opportunity to form the atmosphere in which the recesses of the heart of youth are sought out and the springs of resolution are moved. It is an enlarged home and the opportunity for informal contact is manifold. Around the formal public worship and the work of the classroom is created an atmosphere which may be alive with messages. The Church has all manner of men and women within it. They gather at family dinners. They meet with youth at Communion breakfasts. Many an older man is admired and imitated without his knowledge; but his unconscious influence is none the less potent. Friendships between young and old spring up because age unites as well as divides. The man of ideals and accomplishment walks along the street with his young friend, and as they talk their hearts burn within them like the disciples on the road to Emmaus. In the alert parish the faculty of the church school meets with its students informally and often, and the intellectual vigor of the classroom gives good background for mental exchange and spiritual communion. In the converted parish the Spirit has many openings.

So the national department of my Church is emphasizing the conversion of half-Christians into whole Christians. In its parish life conferences and in its laboratories it is considering what the religious life is and what parish objectives should be. No longer does a parish measure itself simply in terms of attendance, the size of the church school, the number of guilds, or the missionary offerings, important as these things are. It is examining the fundamental aims of parish life and asking, "What are we here for?" Out of this effort have come thousands of people who are, to use the current phrase, really "concerned." Their influence permeates the whole body.

Such an atmosphere goes deep below the level of reason to the inner motivations of the heart. As we have endeavored to show, truth is personal and deep must speak to deep. The parish has an unrivalled opportunity to address the whole man. When parishes everywhere have this combination of joyous worship, of intellectual zeal, and of informal influence, the public schools may well surrender to them the burden of moral education and of social adjustment.

This is the kind of parish which makes over and sustains the home life of its people. Discordant families, drawn within the group, feel the effect of it. They are softened and inspired through the power of mass suggestion, and they change. Only a converted congregation has this power to exorcise evil spirits and to let the true Master of the home come in.

There is new emphasis on the time allowed for education in the formal classroom sense. It is ridiculous to think that any teacher can accomplish much in half an hour a week, a part of which time is spent in calling the roll and getting started (not to mention the interruptions from strolling secretaries). The new insistence demands at least fifty minutes for uninterrupted instruction. This is little enough, and so the movement for weekday sessions on released public school time is gaining in strength. This all shows that even with the present curriculum the Church must have more time for its job. If the Church is to broaden its curriculum to include the subjects outlined in Chapter 6, the whole subject of its legitimate claim on the pupils' time will have to be reviewed.

Up to this point, in drawing attention to the favorable signs, we have paid attention only to the excellent work of our national leaders. But this would not have been possible had there not been a grass-roots response. On the local level the effort has been enormous in comparison with what was considered adequate only a few years ago. Local parishes are giving the church school a priority it has never had before. Attendance figures indicate one result of this new evaluation. In the Episcopal Church the number of teachers and officers has jumped from 46,-336 in 1945 to 99,270 in 1958, and the attendance of pupils from 394,456 to 824,353. For the Church as a whole (excluding the Roman Catholic statistics) and for approximately the same period, the number of teachers has increased from 1,711,595 to 3,350,690, and the number of pupils enrolled from 21,426,453 to 35,692,378.

The increase in numbers has been accompanied by much new building construction. Old parish houses, which were never built with education in mind, are being replaced by modern educational buildings with standard classrooms in order to give teachers a fighting chance.

Millions have been spent in this manner although, alas, too many of the old and inadequate buildings still remain. It is easier now to get church people to give money for religious education than for any other project.

While a full-blown program of religious education—including the allied subjects of history, philosophy, and literature—is obviously possible only in the future, it does not follow that many things cannot be done at the present time which will prepare the way. There is no reason why a modest start at a broader curriculum may not be effected in many parishes right now. All that is needed is the desire to do so and the capacity to look about a bit. The ingenious pastor can probably find some one person in his community who could teach one of these subjects to a Sunday morning group of senior high school students. It might be that the pastor himself would be up to it; or there may be a competent high school teacher in the congregation. Or, perhaps, there may be a college man who majored in philosophy before he began to sell bonds. If the congregation is in a college town, a religiously orientated faculty member might be prevailed upon. Let the pastor take inventory in the community.

If he finds someone to teach philosophy, he might say to him something like this: "I want you to give this class a run-down on the history of philosophy, translating philosophical jargon into the vernacular. Before the year is over I want you to show them what a Christian philosophy is and how, on the level of reason alone, other philosophies—especially the modern ones of meaninglessness—may be met on their own ground." This idea may appeal to some capable person; and if he has any teaching ability, the results might well be startling.

Or, a teacher of literature whom the rector has rounded up might give a similar class a taste of the best Christian literature and poetry, including the Christian classics we previously mentioned. This person must be warned against being a technician or mechanic in literature; he must feel free to squeeze out the last drop of the author's meaning. Taught from such a perspective, and with no holds barred, the class will be entranced.

The most excitement, however, might be found in a class on God's relation to universal history about which there is a growing literature—Butterfield's book *Christianity and History* being one of the latest. If well taught, such a class would have to stretch both its intellectual and spiritual muscles.

Test flights like these here and there would be both stimulated and helped if our national leaders would begin to produce textbooks dealing with Christianity in its relation to the great humanities of which we have been speaking. In the Episcopal Church such books would be a valuable addition to *The Church's Teaching* series. These books do not need to wait for any major change in our church school program. They would guide pilot teachers and classes and would serve to get the whole Church thinking. They are needed now.

Our leaders can take one more action which need not wait on future events, though it would prepare the way for them. It is vitally necessary that both clergy and people become acquainted with modern educational theory, both secular and religious. There is a newborn zeal in this country about school affairs, but it is not, as St. Paul says, "according to knowledge." Stokes tells us that we have a "pathetic" confidence in our public schools, yet we have known little about them. Public and private discussions are conducted with only a modicum of knowledge about the principles involved, and the needle of opinion swings violently from one side to the other. Prejudice enters in, and strong and sometimes violent convictions are often based on minor incidents. The American public, and especially its church people, must learn the ABC's of this great subject.

The need for a diffusion of real knowledge among the body politic is not confined to educational matters alone. It is true, as well, in the realm of theology. The clergy, in the main, have treated the subject matter taught in seminaries as a sort of esoteric knowledge, an arcanum, into which the generality have not the wit to enter, even if they have the right. As a matter of fact, there are people in many congregations today who have had a better education and possess better minds than their clerical leaders. These people are not only capable of entering into theological discussion: they would be intensely interested in it once the velvet curtain were removed. In the Christian Reformed Church, with which I had contact in Grand Rapids, Michigan, the people have been introduced to theology, and carpenters gravely discuss last Sunday's sermon as they eat their lunch. Their religion means much to them, perhaps because it is a part of the Calvinist tradition to take its people into its confidence.

We have had enough moral homilies and topical sermons: let the clergy give us some real meat!

The doctors have come to rely on a general dissemination of the principles of hygiene, and the health of our people has benefited thereby. But illustrations need not be multiplied. One of the great needs in this crisis of education is an informed and intelligent public opinion on the issues involved in religious and secular policy. As the one institution which has a residual responsibility for all education, the Church has the duty to inform its members, not merely as churchmen but as citizens. These people are voters and members of school boards, and they must have a balanced knowledge of the real issues involved. It is the duty of the Church to see to it that immediate steps are taken to share this mystery of educational theory which both religious and secular experts have evolved, so that our churchman-citizens may perform their duties intelligently. They should know the claims of the traditionalists, as well as those of the radicals, as each group has something to contribute. They should be able to appraise for themselves what the various advocates have to say. They must evaluate the present tendency in public school operation toward emphasis on social adjustment, the project method, and vocational training. They should be able to weigh the potential church contribution to the total educational process and to consider intelligently such questions as the division of time.

It is hardly necessary to add that an intelligent and independent public opinion would be of the utmost value to the public school system in very definite and direct ways. For one thing, these people, devoted both to the public schools and to the Church would magnify the vocation of teacher as well as that of minister. Too long has the Church been oblivious to the problem of attracting the best of its youth to this classic calling. It should be as much concerned about the quality of the teacher who trains its youth as it is about the minister who stands in its pulpit. The Churches should also award teachers, especially new ones, that social recognition which is their due and is often denied. These leaders of our children should be invited into the homes of our people instead of being the forgotten men and women of our towns. Too long have many of them been treated like second class citizens and have almost perished from loneliness. The aroused conscience on educational matters should express itself in demanding adequate salaries, salaries at least equal to those of the stone masons and carpenters who build the school buildings! This means supporting the school budget. An aroused and intelligent public opinion would call for an intensive study of the ideals and methods of our teachers' colleges. If the choicest of our youth are to go into teaching, there must be not merely social recognition of a great profession and adequate salaries but also the best possible training. From all accounts our teachers' colleges need, in addition to strong public support, a dose of intelligent criticism. They have been off in a corner long enough.

In other words, educational theory and practice should be added to the broadening curriculum of the Church as it adjusts itself to the conditions of the present age. It is the duty, therefore, of Church leaders to produce textbooks dealing with education in its totality and to urge the formation of adult study groups in this field. Such an effort need not be delayed. Indeed, it brooks no delay if wise decisions are to be made.

In the next chapter we shall consider a possible blueprint of the future. It does no harm to look ahead.

CHAPTER 8

Future Objectives

Abraham went into the unknown not knowing whither he went, but he saw a city. So, education may not know the exact topography of the "south country" where it is to receive an inheritance, but it must venture into new paths with an idea of ultimate values and aims. The outline of the city must have a certain definiteness.

One of the first matters to be considered is the division of time to be allowed to secular and religious education. There are only so many hours in the day, only so many days in the week. The home, the community, free time for recreation and special interests, are a part of the picture. The Church finds that it is pushed for time even with its present curriculum. If it has been proved that the curriculum should be broadened, the crisis becomes acute.

One hour of released time outside the school building (now allowed by the Supreme Court in the case of Zorach *vs*. Clausen) is certainly not sufficient. An hour or more a day *after* public school, as practiced in certain communities by the Jewish Church, puts a heavy burden on the children. The use of Saturday morning for religious instruction robs youth of the one day which should be flexible and free. With the shortened workweek many fathers have Saturday at home, giving the well-disposed a chance to get to know their children. But, in addition, the educational scheme must leave youth some time merely to be itself, to live in its own world. It is not good for children to feel the hot breath of supervision blowing down their necks without let-up. Formal education can suffocate the creative spirit. In simpler times young people had to think up for themselves things to do, and it was the best kind of education. The writer can still remember how, with a few friends after school, he used to dash out into the back lot to build a little house, or "shanty" as we called it. If we had to forage for boards and nails, no harm was done. We were doing something and a part of the joy was that we were doing it on our own. No older person had suggested that we could make a project out of building a house; no one furnished us with money and material from the school budget. No one said that we could use the project to learn carpentry, or the lumber business, or arithmetic. If they had done so, all of the fun would have gone out of it. This was our own idea and it gave us a sense of accomplishment. The capacity of youth to educate itself is astonishing, and both Church and State should give it a chance.

So far as formal education is concerned the only solution I can see is for the nation and the community (the only real authority) to grant the Church one full school day a week for its own use. One objection to released time is that the public school still retains control. This is not a dignified or worthy arrangement. The Church has the right to claim an adequate segment of the child's working time for its very own without having the uneasy and sometimes critical public school authorities in the background. Apart from this fundamental philosophy, the whole operation is messy. Mechanically it is not easy to excuse pupils at certain hours to attend "the church of their choice." The whole school program has to be adjusted so that they may be released during the time given to less essential subjects. About this question as to what is essential and what is non-essential opinions within the school faculty may vary. The fine arts teacher or the music teacher or the band-master may not like it; and the problem of getting the pupils in and out of the room causes confusion, to say nothing of the problem of transportation. I know from personal experience that parents who have to provide this transportation are often driven to distraction. In the background is that lingering sense of responsibility which the public schools feel for the whole operation. The Church, when it is ready to do so, must claim sufficient time for its own purposes as its inalienable right.

To this additional increment of time provided by one day a week, there must be a concentration in space. It is obvious that the individual congregations constituting the Church could not provide the full-fledged curriculum which the new program calls for. The church people in any given town would have to cooperate in erecting an adequate building (or buildings) to which all of the pupils would go at the same time. On Sunday, of course, all would repair to their own churches. This would provide a clear cut solution to the problem.

Psychologically, the effect on the pupils themselves would be excellent. Released time for religious training makes religion seem like another subject—like taking piano lessons. Dashing away to some church for an hour may be welcomed as a lark, but the massive public school seems like real business in comparison. To give one day a week to religion and allied subjects in a dignified manner, to have an adequate building, for this regular period, to instill the sense of corporate interest in both pupils and teachers, and to combine all these impressions with the feeling that this is important—this would tend to produce a change of attitude. Religion would no longer seem like an option, or even one subject among many, but rather as something basic to all the rest.

The study of the humanities allied to the central tradition would not only deepen the religious imprint, but also help to integrate the ideas of religion with the public school curriculum. No student could take the courses in philosophy, history, and literature without a change of attitude toward all study. These courses would provide the natural link between the Bible and the learning of the day. Now the connecting links are tenuous indeed, and the Bible—universal as it is—seems a book apart. We must have a modulation from the study of the Scriptures to other studies; and this such a school could provide. Here, again, we can see the close, though informal, relationship which this type of school would have with secular education. This modulation would be like the quality of mercy which blesses him that gives and him that takes.

The work in this school would be different in character from that attempted in the various churches on Sunday. On Sunday, in each individual church, the emphasis would be on worship and only secondarily on instruction. On Wednesday, for example, it would be on instruction, with worship taking an important, but secondary, place. On Sunday the Bible would be studied for its spiritual message to the individual; its call to commitment would be emphasized. Personal religion and its aid in solving the problems of youth would be in the ascendant. On Wednesday mental discipline would have the priority.

Youth needs to develop its powers through the training of the intellect. The young must master a subject as well as think of personal problems. It needs the drudgery and the rugged task of application to *content*. Only so can horizons be broadened and the glance of spirit be lifted to matters which transcend the personal. It must learn what thoroughness means, if the mind is ever to be capable of original thought. The deep emphasis of this school would not be on conformity or social adjustment, but on creativity. Sunday should give the discovery of individual mission. Wednesday should give mental power full play.

In our outline of possible future developments we envisage, therefore, a church private school in each community, but a private school teaching only those studies which reveal the meaning of life. All of the subjects necessary to basic education would be left to the public schools.

Not only the value of, but the imperative need for, the full-time private school in our country's educational plan have been amply demonstrated. In many places, and for a variety of reasons, parents feel obliged to send their children to private schools if they can afford to do so. They think that they are confronted by a condition, not a theory, and they are going to do the best they can for their offspring. However, the established private full-time schools are rooted in good democratic theory which is opposed to monopoly in education as well as in economics. We must preserve the idea of healthy competition, and it is not well for the State to control the entire educational process either on the college level or in the grades. The private schools offer to our people, at least to those in a certain economic strata, the power of choice. While their limited number deprives them of universal usefulness to all groups, it is still the custom of the best of them to provide scholarships so that able young people from any economic level can attend.

The private schools enjoy a freedom denied to the public schools in the formation of a curriculum. In an earlier chapter mention was made of the pressures to which public school superintendents and principals are subjected by various groups. This sort of unintelligent compulsion does not exist in private schools, whose boards of trustees are much more likely to be of one mind.

Because of this freedom these schools can and do serve as laboratories of educational procedure which exert a profound influence on the public school world. It was in the private school that the first attempt was made to give courses to able students for which college credit would be allowed. The practice has now been followed in some of the best high schools which do not hesitate to acknowledge their debt to the private school in this, and in many other ways. We need two eyes looking at the same thing from different angles if we are to perceive *depth,* and this is just as true in education as it is in optics.

The rate at which full-time private schools are growing is a phenomenon which deserves some study. In the Episcopal Church the movement has attained its greatest impetus in Florida and California; but in many other parts of our country it is also gaining momentum. A parish starts a nursery school and then a kindergarten, perhaps because the public schools do not provide such services. Under pressure from the parents it adds an additional grade each year. This is not to say that in any given instance this may not have been justified; certainly some outstanding schools have resulted from the process. It is a curious commentary on the situation, by the way, to see how willing, if not eager, parents are to send their children to private schools of any description. Sometimes it is done because of social considerations; but in the main it is because they think that in the private school their progeny will receive a better education. The public school may have all of the plush features described in Chapter 2, but these are surrendered without a qualm—certainly an indication of their unimportance as criteria in making a choice.

It may be that the establishment of full-time private schools across the nation, after the example of the Roman Catholic Church and others, will be the solution adopted by the church people of America. But I hope that there is another answer. One result would be that the public and private schools would, in the main, cater to different classes with a consequent spiritual loss.

What I am proposing is a compromise which, I believe, would preserve the essential values of both institutions. If the private school has the values I have described, it should be in every community, and not just here and there. In other words, monopoly should be broken everywhere. The one-day-a-week private school under church auspices, with its curriculum limited to those subjects which best convey meaning, would be a real school, free to follow its own genius and with an ethos of its own. But it would leave to the public school all the elements of a sound basic education. All of the pupils in the town would go to both schools between which there would be a close but informal relationship. This is a far cry from attempting to parallel the entire public school system with full-time church schools; but it would introduce everywhere a new and needed element into education.

While the consummation of this objective awaits the interplay of many minds and the processes of time, it is none too soon to consider the objections which will be raised. It is highly probable that public school people and many others will say that the public schools simply cannot spare a day a week. To their minds the idea will seem fantastic. In answer to this it must be said that from the outset this book has taken the position that the public schools must draw in their reins. Probably with good will, but under group pressure and with fuzzy thinking, they have taken on function after function which does not belong to them. Much that has been done is not worthy to be called education and can be sloughed off without hurt to any essential function. There is no need to review here what has been said in earlier chapters; it is enough to state that the public schools of this country waste an enormous amount of time and money. By concentrating on what is essential and by doing what no one else can do, they can easily accomplish in four days what they now attempt to accomplish in five. The Church can make much better use of that time.

Another objection will come from Church people who will say that the cost of such a plan would be prohibitive. Others do not think so. Members of the Roman Catholic, the Christian Reformed, and the Missouri Synod Lutheran Churches are willing to go to the much greater expense of paralleling the public school system with full-time private schools of their own; and, in addition, they pay the regular school taxes. The expense of the cooperative effort here suggested would be moderate in comparison with that borne by millions of other earnest church people. The money potential is there and it is not too much to expect that, with a drastic reduction of public school superfluities, the swollen school taxes could be reduced.

Another objection by church people might be that an adequate faculty could not be provided on a one-day-a-week, voluntary basis. At the present time this would surely present a major difficulty; but here we are attempting to outline a future objective. Reference has already been made to the progress in teacher training. When this program gets into full operation there will be a sufficient number of volunteers who will give one day a week to teaching as their reasonable service to God. Many young college-bred business men and women will qualify for teaching, if the training is made available and the challenge given with a sufficient sense of urgency. In the potential contribution of the college world we find an enormous resource which as yet has only partially been tapped, although many college people are now teaching Sunday mornings. There is an incredible waste now on the college level because so many men and women who majored in one of the great humanities drop all connection with them upon graduation. It is true, of course, that the college world exerts a broad cultural influence and this residual atmosphere tends to make graduates more responsible citizens. But it is a distinct loss to society not to be able to provide those who have the teaching instinct (as many have) with the opportunity to teach *part time* in the subject which so interested them in undergraduate years. The proposed broadening of the Church's curriculum would offer them the opportunity to grow in their intellectual life—and we all know that the best way to master a subject is to teach it.

If any proof were needed that a great many college graduates would welcome such an opening, it is furnished by the increasing number of men, even of middle age, who, having rejected a call to the ministry in their youth, have felt the constant nagging of the Spirit. In many cases they have dropped everything to go to theological school in order to prepare for ordination. In the same way the Spirit is whispering to many that they can teach; but how to manage it is the question. They must keep on with their business. So the part-time private church school, which is here recommended, points the way to a solution. These men and women can devote one weekday, or the part of one weekday, to teaching—not only Bible but also philosophy, history or literature, following their special interests. It is not too much to expect that an awakened business world would give them the opportunity to do so.

However, this is not the whole story. There will be clergy, professional people of various sorts, and religiously orientated public school teachers who will respond to an opportunity worthy of their talents. A few such schools begun in places where conditions are favorable would lead the way and others would follow. It can be done. The Church need simply call upon its reserve teaching power.

It will be asked whether or not it would be an economic waste to construct a building which would be in operation only one day a week. As I envisage such an institution, it would be in constant use. Adult study classes of all sorts could be held in the evenings. Community institutions, such as the Boy Scouts and Girl Scouts could have their headquarters in such a building. Lectures could be given during the daytime and in many other ways it could meet community needs.

Another objection may be that the Church could not make provision for young people who have no church connection. This question will bear careful examination. The total number of boys and girls enrolled in our public schools is about 34,000,000. The total number of pupils enrolled in all non-Roman Catholic Sunday schools reaches the astonishing figure of 35,692,378 according to the National Council of Churches. The discrepancy in the figures may be accounted for by the fact that such statistics cannot be always perfectly accurate, or because there are many nursery and kindergarten classes conducted by the Church in areas where they are not provided by the public schools. However, the figures are certainly accurate enough to show that the Church has contact with an enormous segment of the country's youth. The Jewish people would undoubtedly welcome this extra day and would make excellent use of it. Splinter groups, hostile to the Church, would have to be provided for by the community in some manner. These people have their rights; but the enormous number of children and young people already connected with the Church have rights too, of which they should not be deprived by the antagonisms of minorities.

There are other objections which at once come to mind —such as the difficulty caused by state public school laws which require a certain number of school days each year. The longer school term, working so successfuly in Rochester, Minnesota, might offer one approach to the problem. In any case, an aroused public opinion could handle this difficulty.

So here are the problems, the suggested solution, and some of the probable objections. What the future may bring forth no man can tell. If this book has given food for thought along new lines I shall feel that its mission has been accomplished. It is certain, however, that the Church has a heavy responsibility in future educational developments; it cannot evade this responsibility. It must pick up the burden it once laid down. It has the power to do so.

Has it the will?

CHAPTER 9

The Science of Sciences

This book, strictly speaking, ends with the previous chapter. Any one who has read that far has discovered its essential message and may put the book down. However, the responsibility of the Church in education does not end with the first twelve grades in school. There remains the ultimate task of interpreting all knowledge.

We speak of the conflict of religion and science, thinking perhaps that this is a thing of the past. Yet the reconciling word in that conflict has not yet been said. We talk of peace when there is no peace. Israel may be quiet for forty years, each man living under his own vine and fig tree, but then the same old trouble begins, perhaps from a new quarter. Just now our projected excursions into interplanetary space have stirred things up all over again. The stars used to appeal to our mystic sense; but now, while the prospect of a trip to Venus excites us, the old glamour of mystery has disappeared. Khrushchev says that there are no angels in space; but while we dismiss the statement as superficial, there is a residual fear that penetration into space, like penetration into the atom, may reveal the fact that there is no God. If that happens, even immensity becomes commonplace and dreary.

This is, of course, just an extension of the conflict which has existed for a long time between the tangible things of sense and the intangibles which alone protect the values man has always held dear. St. Paul speaks of the struggle when he says that the things which are seen are temporal while the things which are unseen are eternal. The tendency to identify meaning with matter is not a new one; the issue has merely taken a dramatic turn. The Church is only fighting a rear-guard action when people begin to fear that greatness in belief and conduct rests on the insecure foundations of myth, fable, and wishful thinking.

On balance, and in spite of the fact that numbers of scientists are Christians, the weight of scientific opinion falls on the side of a naturalistic explanation of the universe. Science has conferred untold benefits, but at the same time it constitutes a threat not only to physical life on this planet but also to man's spiritual and intellectual powers.

Strange as it may seem, science threatens the creative intellect as a common possession of men. No one can deny that along sharply defined and narrow lines science has produced dedicated intellectual effort—almost a new kind of man. This man's knowledge along the line of his specialty is positively frightening. Yet the very prestige of science makes the average man feel a lessening of responsibility because he thinks that only an intellectually elite can understand the intricate mathematical, physical, or chemical problems involved. The temptation is to feel that science is the new messiah and that only the other fellow can understand its mysteries. "Let George do it" is a motto which has many applications.

The method of science puts up roadblocks to good thinking, even in the scientific world itself. The very genius of science is to attempt to understand by subdivision just as we take a machine apart to see how it works. When science faces a complicated problem, it promptly proceeds to break it down into simpler elements. Reasonable as this process is, it involves a change in the scale of observation which handicaps thinking about the original problem. A threshold has been crossed and the steps cannot be retraced. For instance, water can be separated into hydrogen and oxygen but by no possible chance can we, having only hydrogen and oxygen to deal with, learn anything about the characteristics of water. Some vital link has been lost in the process.

If we would understand the laws governing human society, science says that we must subdivide at once and study the individual man. But the moment we do this we cross a threshold which leads us farther and farther from our original objective. Again, we can subdivide and go on to a study of the human body; but now we cross another threshold which leads us still farther astray, for no study of physiology or anatomy or bio-chemistry can possibly help us to a knowledge of the individual, to say nothing of mass psychology. The scientific method sets up barriers to constructive thinking and at the same time fools us by its atmosphere of omniscience.

The last plunge made by science is into the sub-atomic and here the hocus pocus is truly astounding, for we are

now introduced into a different world altogether: we
have got beyond the realm of cause and effect. Our deepest instincts tell us that this is a universe, but here at the
very bottom of the barrel we seem to find something
dashing around without rhyme or reason; so we are told
that this is not a universe but a multiverse. Nothing can
be depended upon to act in an orderly manner. All we
can count on is the amount of probability. Two and two
only probably make four. It is said that here comes the
great plunge out of the universe, as we have been taught
to conceive it, into a vast unknown where there is no order, no law and—most ominous of all—no meaning. This
plunge has been compared with religious conversion
which may do violence to one's ingrained habits of
thought as he makes this thorough inner orientation.
This threshold is surely not the entrance into Paradise
but into Hell. It is difficult to conceive anything which
would do more to dry up the springs of the intellectual
life than this doctrine of meaninglessness. One can quite
understand the remark that literature was invented to
take our minds off the universe of the scientists.

Finally, each branch of science tends to come up with
its own brand of superstition. In his book, *The Road to
Reason,* the late Comte du Nouy writes as follows:

In this book I have tried to show that though the observations of science are solid, its interpretations are sometimes
fragile. My sole aim in doing so was to warn laymen against
the scientific mysticism that does not withstand an honest
examination, but that some people have tried to turn into a
weapon against spiritual mysticism. Scientific superstition,

like all superstition, derives its prestige in part from the ignorance of the crowd. It must not be allowed to keep a free man from thinking freely.[1]

Here we have it in the words of a man who was himself a distinguished scientist. On the basis of a narrow ledge of fact and by dint of ruling out all other facts, some scientists and a gang of camp followers have the effrontery to tell free men what they must, and what they must not, think about the meaning of life and the vast problems of human existence. We are indeed, as Pollard said, living in a new dark age, and like people in all dark ages, we do not know it.[2]

So while science has stimulated human thought in some areas, in others it has dried up the mental springs by minimizing and pooh-poohing uncongenial facts—particularly the facts which are the data of the science of theology. No human endeavor has suffered more from this assault on the depth and dignity of human nature than the public schools, because the public school theorists have, in the main, abjectly surrendered to the prestige, the method, and the superstitions of science, crying out in modern terms, "Great is Diana of the Ephesians!"

Strange as it may seem, all of this raises no new problem in human affairs. On a lesser stage and with fewer actors, the western world has gone through precisely this same crisis before. It was brought about by the discovery of the classics of antiquity in the thirteenth century—

[1] Toronto: Longman's Green and Co., 1955, p. 224. Used by permission.

[2] *The Christian Idea of Education*, p. 14.

particularly in the writings of the philosopher-scientists of the Greeks. This precipitated the first collision between the Church and what might be called the beginnings of the modern scientific method. For twelve centuries the Church had had but little touch with the external world of nature as contributory to its basic philosophy. Pegis, in his introduction to *The Basic Writings of St. Thomas Aquinas,* describes the predicament as follows:

For centuries Christian thought had learned and meditated on the grammar of the love of God. But in the presence of Greek philosophy those who had hitherto spoken the language of supernatural devotion were called upon to learn, in addition, the natural language of reason seeking to understand the world and itself. Early medieval thinkers knew the world more as "worldliness" than as "reality." Being devout masters of the interior life they knew only the world which they could build within their search for the vision of God. Such a world was an interior castle of perfection, a spiritual mirror, in which each soul might experience the mystery of the divine love. But when we go from the twelfth century of St. Bernard to the thirteenth century of St. Thomas, we meet the world in all of its reality, we meet reason in all of its naturalness, we meet the wisdom so eminently embodied in Aristotle, which is the connatural work and vision of the human reason.*

With the discovery of Aristotle, and the other Greek scientist-philosophers, Christian thought had a rude shock, for these men philosophized on the basis of what they had actually observed of the working of nature. While Christian thought, on the basis of revelation, worked from the top down, Greek thought with the aid of human reason worked from the bottom up. The

* Quoted with permission of Random House, Inc.

Greeks felt that they could prove what they asserted. Aristotle made some deductions from his observations which implicitly challenged the Christian faith; in the long run, unless disproved, they would have destroyed it as a figment of the imagination. It was true, of course, that other deductions of Aristotle were capable of becoming bulwarks of the faith. The difficulty was that the unpleasant deductions had to be disposed of by human reason and not by revelation. Facts had to be met with facts, reason with better reason. The man who met this challenge was St. Thomas Aquinas.

This remarkable man did not flinch from this sharp testing of his mental powers. Despite his entirely different background he made himself intimately acquainted with this formidable personage of the past. He mastered his method and his science and then met him on his own grounds. St. Thomas has been called an Aristotelian; but that is true only in the sense that he accepted in Aristotle what seemed to him impregnable from a reasonable standpoint, while disposing of the rest. He accomplished a synthesis for his time between the thought of the Church and the best science of the day. The result was that science became the bulwark and ally of the Christian Church.[3]

[3] This is not to imply that Thomism is necessarily the modern answer to the challenge of science. Aristotle represented the scientific method and approach. His thought could only be met on its own ground and that is what Aquinas did. The Church of the twentieth century must meet the goliath of science where it is and use the same weapons.

It is illuminating to learn that Pythagoras in the sixth century

History does repeat itself. Now, seven hundred years later, the same battle is raging on a wider field and with even greater intensity. The conflict is more complicated and confusing than the one St. Thomas had to endure, for if he had one great antagonist, now the foe is legion. Yet what is inevitable must have the seeds of good in it, and we still have resiliency enough to see that this phenomenon is a familiar one; this same battle was fought and won long ago, and large as the action is, it is still only a mopping up operation.

Anyone who would attempt the task of St. Thomas in the face of modern science, would have, first of all, to deal with different branches of knowledge. It would be useless for the Church to consider the philosophical deductions of any one specialty, for this specialty's very isolation from other disciplines produces a certain distortion of its

B.C. was deeply interested in this same attempt to reconcile religious experience with the intellectual life. Speaking of the Orphic sects, John Baillie writes as follows: "Their purpose was the worship of Dionysus but what specially characterizes them is the peculiar mingling of a strong intellectual interest with this devotional one. A generation previously Greek science and philosophy had together been born in the Ionian colonies and now the great Pythagoras was carrying on this tradition in the colonies of Southern Italy. In the thought of Pythagoras the scientific tradition on the one hand and the Dionysiac religion on the other seem to be fused in a single whole. How far Pythagoras was the founder of Orphism and how far he was influenced by Orphic sects still existing it is now very difficult to say; but it is certain that the Pythagorean fusion of interests is reflected to a large extent in the Orphic movement as a whole." Quoted from John Baillie's *And the Life Everlasting* (New York: Charles Scribner's Sons, 1933) page 128. Used by permission.

facts. The division of knowledge into different areas is in itself a concession to human frailty. It is for convenience only, but it should always be remembered that the division is arbitrary after all. It does not take an expert to see that one study merges into another and can only be understood in relation to that which is beyond itself. This is a universe after all, no matter how hard we try to tear it apart. Einstein held this faith to the end, and I will go along with him and the common sense of mankind in the matter. Yet, while it is generally agreed that knowledge is one because the universe is one, it is not easy to arrest the centrifugal tendency and to make it centripetal instead. These divisions, artificial though they may be, are stubborn things, and there are those who guard the ramparts of each one. One department of the university eyes another, and it is whispered that even top professors do not like to mingle and discuss relationships for fear of betraying ignorance. The professor stands on an uneasy pedestal.

Stubborn as the difficulty may be, however, there are few who would deny that there should be a "science of sciences" which would reverse this process of endless division. It is confusing and annoying to have a corporal's guard, with cutlasses and derringers, standing watch over their minute subject. One would think that, like the Forty-Niners in California, they had a claim on that bit of intellectual territory. There is a loss in all of this because it would be helpful to see what is important and what is less important; it would be illuminating to have some branches of knowledge given the place to which they are entitled after having had to sit in the seat of the humble; it would be exciting to see a grander picture emerge, if there could be a scale of values—in other words, to repeat, a "Science of Sciences."

In Cullen's book, *The Imperial Intellect*, an account is given of how John Henry Newman struggled with this same question at Oxford in the first part of the last century. In Newman's earlier days at Oriel College there were so few basic subjects that he believed one tutor could integrate and teach them all. With this method the student would get everything in due proportion from the tutor who would also, as an added responsibility, attend to the young man's religious instruction. Nothing could be more unified than that! With the growing number of subjects, as new disciplines came along, this particular method of integration proved to be impossible. His next step, years later, when he became head of what was to become the Catholic University of Ireland, was to see if he could find some person to develop the "science of sciences," by mastering each subject and then assigning it to its proper place in a symphony of learning. This might have been possible—Newman himself felt up to it—but he could not find the man and the project was abandoned. Newman, by the way, did not consider that theology was the "Queen of the Sciences" in the sense that the members of the theological faculty could order the others about or assign them their places at the table of learning. Theology, to him, was just one of the sciences, although, of course, it dealt with high matters. Newman believed in academic freedom.

So the idea that the university itself could unify knowledge had to be given up, and Newman lived to see countless new courses added to the curriculum without any hope that any power within the academic world could be found which could assign them their proper place in the universe of knowledge. The same difficulty exists today.

This incurs a double loss. There is a loss to knowledge itself, for specialization is self-defeating in the long run. No fact can be isolated, like a fish on the dock, and remain unchanged. From each fact filaments of relationship stream forth to the entire universe. Arbitrarily to limit the relationship of fact to fact is to take liberties with the fact and to cast doubt upon its "factness." Then there is the loss to interpretation. Unless a fact can be seen in its universal relationship, no universal deduction can be drawn from it. Yet this is exactly what some men of science have tried to do—yielding to that innate thirst for *meaning* which resides in each human soul. It seems both pathetic and ironical that the deeper they plunge into the womb of the universe, the more the conviction grows within them that the only meaning is that there is no meaning at all.

When there is a log jam in the river, it often may be just one log which causes all the trouble. So when a situation presents what seems to be an insoluble problem, some slight move may solve the difficulty. The key to the present intellectual log jam might well be an institution, free from both State and Church domination, which would devote itself to the "science of sciences" and to the great task of interpretation. In this "college" (I search for the right word) theology would have to be recognized as one of the sciences, because on this science rests the ultimate burden. Theology has its own data which has the same right to be accepted as fact as that of any other discipline. It has its feet firmly planted in history and can claim that it carries anthropology to its ultimate deductions. It is rooted in the nature of the soul of man and is, therefore, the true existentialism, completing the studies of the psychiatrist. Theology must claim a new academic recognition.

In this atmosphere of intellectual freedom, controlled only by the conviction that the truth is one, the task of the theological members of this "circle" would be gradually to acquaint themselves with the meaningful elements in every field of knowledge, even as Aquinas did in mastering the science of his day. They would represent the Church in its new found determination to find out for itself what these new, and oftentimes disturbing, disciplines are all about and to consider them in relation to the Christian revelation. They would look on facts with a new eye, rejecting no fact as *fact,* but including the higher centers of man as data worthy of consideration in their relationship to these facts. They would accompany man through each dark tunnel of the soul as he crosses threshold after threshold in the search for meaning. The Church must, in a sense, take the plunge with man— feel the force of each argument, even to the peril of its own soul. Only so will it achieve the power to rescue man from an intellectual, as well as a moral, abyss. There is no easy way. The Church will doubtless feel that it will endure anything rather than this proposed agony of thinking. But Aquinas endured the agony, and the ultimate result of the encounter of Christian theology with the science of the thirteenth century was to strengthen the Church with a new intellectual fiber. So it can be today. Man's intelligence is not meant to be at war with his spiritual powers, for man is one as the universe is one. *If the Church, even at this late date and in spite of generations of intellectual laziness, will make the effort to "read, mark, learn, and inwardly digest" the various disciplines which are engaging the human mind, it will find that they are on the side of man's best self and can add immeasurably to his spiritual stature.*

Just how this idea would assume form and substance, how it could have a local habitation and a name, I shall not venture to say. In itself, the thought is a simple one. As in the days of David the wood and the stone are lying about. Perhaps the Temple will some day be built.

This institution, college—call it what you will—could be the most creative and exciting phenomenon in American intellectual life. It would produce a new kind of scholar, the kind Newman was looking for and could not find. The ramifications of its influence would help to cure the intellectual hardening of the arteries which afflicts the academic world. At the same time it would infuse the new unity of knowledge with the spirit of religion which, without controlling, would still illumine the academic effort with the radiance of the Eternal.